Regulating Foreign Direct Investment for Development

This book offers a comprehensive overview of the relationship between Foreign Direct Investment (FDI) regulation and sustainable development in Bangladesh.

It is widely accepted that FDI-induced development is essential for the growth of undeveloped economies, but it can create a conflict between the investors' goal of profit maximisation and the host state's pursuit of economic gains. FDI-induced development is especially important for the economy of Bangladesh, the focus of this book, which argues that a balanced regulatory approach is necessary to ensure that FDI benefits all stakeholders. In examining Bangladesh's FDI regulatory regime, the authors reveal that it is investor-centric and lacks a development-oriented approach. They discuss the relevant laws, practices, mechanisms, and institutions that govern the entrance regulations and incentives for foreign investment, as well as the protection of the environment and human rights, with special attention to labour rights, involuntary displacement, and the protection of both the investors and the state in which they invest. From this analysis, the book recommends reforms to introduce development as a primary goal while maintaining Bangladesh's appeal as an FDI destination.

The book will be of interest to researchers, students, and academics in the fields of economics, politics, sustainable development, and economic growth. It will also be of great interest to FDI strategists, policymakers, negotiators, administrators, and legislators in creating a balanced regulatory regime to attract FDIs for development.

Nakib Mohammad Nasrullah is Professor of Law at the University of Dhaka and the Vice-Chancellor of the Islamic University in Kushtia.

Mia Mahmudur Rahim is Associate Professor of Law at the University of New England and Professor in Residence at the National Law University, Meghalaya.

Routledge Focus on Environment and Sustainability

Global Forest Visualization
From Green Marbles to Storyworlds
Lynda Olman and Birgit Schneider

Sustainable Marketing and the Circular Economy in Poland
Key Concepts and Strategies
Anita Proszowska, Ewa Prymon-Ryś, Anna Kondak, Aleksandra Wilk, and Anna Dubel

Risk Management for Water Professionals
Technical, Psychological and Sociological Underpinnings
Anna Kosovac

Climate Perspectives from the Congo Basin
Bila-Isia Inogwabini

Everyday Agri-Environmental Governance
The Emergence of Sustainability through Assemblage Thinking
Jérémie Forney, Dana Bentia, and Angga Dwiartama

Electric Cars and the Resource Challenge
Theo Henckens

Regulating Foreign Direct Investment for Development
Perspectives from Bangladesh
Nakib Mohammad Nasrullah and Mia Mahmudur Rahim

For more information about this series, please visit: www.routledge.com/Routledge-Focus-on-Environment-and-Sustainability/book-series/RFES

Regulating Foreign Direct Investment for Development

Perspectives from Bangladesh

Nakib Mohammad Nasrullah and Mia Mahmudur Rahim

First published 2025
by Routledge
4 Park Square, Milton Park, Abingdon, Oxon OX14 4RN

and by Routledge
605 Third Avenue, New York, NY 10158

Routledge is an imprint of the Taylor & Francis Group, an informa business

British Library Cataloguing-in-Publication Data
A catalogue record for this book is available from the British Library

ISBN: 978-1-032-74414-8 (hbk)
ISBN: 978-1-032-74416-2 (pbk)
ISBN: 978-1-003-46911-7 (ebk)

DOI: 10.4324/9781003469117

Typeset in Times New Roman
by KnowledgeWorks Global Ltd.

Contents

1 Introduction

1.1 Introduction

In today's globalised economy, foreign direct investment (FDI) is widely recognised as a crucial tool for fostering sustainable economic growth and social development – especially in developing and least developed host countries. The benefits of FDI-induced development include the creation of capital resources, increased gross domestic product (GDP), job creation, poverty reduction, promotion of industrialisation, technology transfer, human resource development and other social advancements. However, these developmental benefits cannot be guaranteed automatically. Relying solely on a liberalised legal framework for FDI entry and operation may not ensure that development occurs alongside an increase in FDI in a host country, and it may even have a negative impact on its socio-economic condition. As a result, it is essential to regulate FDI through legal means in a host country in order to maximise its desired development benefits while minimising its negative impacts. This need for regulation is clearly demonstrated in the context of Bangladesh.

During the post-war era, FDI emerged as an alternative to foreign aid and loans in the global economic and financial practice. This led to a trend of both regulation and liberalisation of FDI in national laws and policies. Initially, regulation policies were introduced by communist countries, which took a restrictive approach towards FDI.[1] They believed that FDI, particularly through foreign multinational corporations (MNCs), created economic dominance over developing host countries and perpetuated a state of dependency on capital-exporting developed countries.[2] On the contrary, European democratic countries and the USA had open and accepting attitudes towards FDI as a means of promoting economic growth.[3] This open attitude began to influence developing countries as well, leading to an increase in FDI inflows in the latter half of the 1980s, driven by the growing popularity of economic liberalism worldwide.[4] Additionally, host countries observed how FDI facilitated the participation of developing and least developed countries in the global production network, leading to increased economic output and welfare.

DOI: 10.4324/9781003469117-1

The prominence of the liberal approach in laws and policies facilitates FDI to enter and operate in host countries. Liberal policies also offered fiscal and non-fiscal incentives to attract and motivate potential investors. Bilateral investment treaties (BITs) between developed countries that exported capital and developing countries that imported capital also greatly influenced national laws and policies regarding FDI. According to the World Investment Report 2001, between 1991 and 2000, approximately 1,185 regulatory changes were introduced in national FDI regimes, of which 1,121 were to create a more favourable environment for FDI.[5] This trend has continued in the first five years of the 21st century. In 2004 alone, 87 per cent of the 271 changes in national investment laws favoured FDI.[6]

The liberalisation of regulation proves to be favourable and attractive to foreign investors in the sense that it creates more opportunities for profit-making from investment at the advantage of lax legal situations in the host country. Conversely, the effect of liberalisation on development appears to be mixed or even proves to be harmful, as it leads to the decrease in the scope of the host country's control over investors in many respects that have development implications. For example, unregulated fiscal and non-fiscal incentives, particularly repatriation and transfer pricing, may affect the tax regulation of a country[7]; the open permission in industrialisation may impact local industries,[8] and it cannot contribute rightly to employment generation and human resource development in the absence of proper labour regulation. In addition, FDI operations may negatively impact a host country's natural environment, labour, human rights and social conditions if strict regulation is absent. Some recent harmful incidents wrought by MNCs in developing countries affecting the environment, natural resources and human rights are attributed to the laxity of FDI regulation, thus contributing to the realisation of the bad impact of liberalisation.[9]

The growing realisation of the ineffectiveness of liberalisation and the need for state control or legal regulation has led to a rethinking of FDI laws and regulations. Additionally, successive economic crises in recent years have led to the rapid withdrawal of capital from host states, further destabilising the weaker economies.[10] As a result, a mixed and balanced form of legislation has emerged with a desire to attract investment on the one hand and to control it on the other.

States that traditionally maintained an open policy regarding the inflow of foreign investment are currently beginning to impose restraints. Some developed countries have introduced screening of foreign investment entry, including stringent reporting requirements. Some developing countries have begun to adopt similar laws in consideration of their economic and social development.[11]

In addition, some scholars and academics have proposed pursuing a regulatory approach in setting FDI laws and policies to protect the interests of host countries. Sornarajah proposes a "middle path".[12] Solomon and Mirsky hold that FDI legislation should be enacted considering some common problems that are significantly related to the development goals of FDI.[13] Seid proposes "regulated openness" of investment regimes where both regulation and openness co-exist in a balanced and pragmatic manner.[14]

Thus the notion of regulation of FDI has now become a reality for the purpose of development in developing and least developed host countries, as there is an in-depth relation between regulation and FDI-induced development. As far as FDI-induced development aspects are concerned, the concept of regulation can encompass them all. Still, most importantly, it involves entry regulation, fiscal and financial regulation, market regulation, environmental regulation, labour regulation and regulation regarding human rights and other social conditions. The regulatory issues must be pursued along with the attractive aspect of liberalisation in core FDI legislations, BITs and other laws that might have implications for the operation of FDI, such as fiscal laws, environmental laws, labour laws, laws relating to occupational safety and health, laws relating to the protection of natural resources, acquisition of land, right to resettlement and property rights. Without integrating regulatory aspects in the legal and policy frameworks, the FDIs will not support the desired developmental goal of FDI in the context of developing host states in general and Bangladesh in particular.

1.2 FDI in Bangladesh

Bangladesh, a least developed country, is beset by multiple economic and social problems. It considers FDI to be a major vehicle for its development. It has striven to attract and increase the inflow of FDI through legal, political and bilateral treaty initiatives to achieve its desired sustainable development goal. The initiatives include the enactment of the *Foreign Private Investment (Promotion and Protection) Act* in 1980, the *Board of Investment Act (currently Bangladesh Investment Development Authority, BIDA) Act* in 1989, the *Bangladesh Export Processing Zones Authority Act* in 1980, the *Bangladesh Private Export Processing Zones Authority Act* in 1996 and the adoption of the *National Industrial Policy (NIP)* in 1982 with periodic modification in every five years. Bangladesh has so far concluded 35 BITs with other states.

The *Foreign Private Investment (Promotion and Protection) Act* (FPIA), as core legislation, offers a legal framework for the protection of FDI, including fair and equitable treatment, equal treatment of foreign and local investments, safeguarding foreign investment from expropriation and assuring the repatriation of finance and profit deriving from share disposal. The *Board of Investment Act* establishes a legal agency to regulate and act as a custodian to facilitate the investment of local and foreign capital. The Bangladesh Export Processing Zones Authority (BEPZA), currently Bangladesh Economic Zones Authority (BEZA), assists foreign companies with plenty of fiscal and non-fiscal initiatives. There are also many other laws and policies in place for the regulation of FDI operations in Bangladesh. They are, for example, company and corporation laws, fiscal law, labour and employment law, laws relating to the acquisition of land, energy law and policies, environmental laws and policies and laws relating to foreign exchange regulation.

Bangladeshi laws and policies adopted so far do not seem to be development-focused on the whole in their application to FDI at either the entry or operation stage. They appear to be mostly focused on offering protection and incentives for investors, lack any specific and binding responsibility regime for investors for the protection of national development interests and have deficiencies as a catalyst for economic and social development in terms of legal provisions and enforcement mechanisms. This is because the FDI-related laws and policies in this country are influenced by the concept of investment facilitation at the desire of investors from capital-exporting developed countries. In different legal aspects affecting FDI operations, development issues such as the increase in national revenue, the protection of labour rights, the protection of the environment and human rights are not given due attention by government policymakers. BITs are almost adopted traditionally simply focusing on the protection of investment, lacking adequate reference to development-oriented aspects.

The desired developmental goal of FDI cannot be achieved in Bangladesh unless it pursues a development-friendly FDI regulatory regime. Thus, there is a scope for an investigation or evaluation of the entire legal regime of FDI to explore (a) whether it serves the developmental interest of Bangladesh and (b) what is essential to establish a development-oriented regulatory framework for FDI operation. The evident absence of any fundamental and original legal research in this area highlights the imperative of this book as a timely reformist response and attempt to remodel the existing legal regime into a development-oriented FDI regulatory framework.

1.3 Scope of the Book

This book is dedicated to the legal regulation of FDI, focusing on core FDI legislation, BITs and other relevant laws in Bangladesh. For this book, legal regulation includes the current state of the law, what we want the law to be, how well it works, how strong and suitable it is and how we ensure people follow it to achieve its purpose.

The book explores the legal framework for Bangladesh as a host nation to control FDI at the entry and post-entry stages in order to achieve its development goals or make it more development-focused. While sustainable development topics are discussed, not all sustainable development challenges are related to FDI regulation. The discussion in the book includes entry regulation, stakeholder interests, environmental regulation and human rights regulation.

Entry regulation depends on the host state's evaluation of investment proposals' potential to drive national economic and social development through industrialisation, employment, international market access, human resource development, capital growth and environmental sustainability. Therefore, the research in this book focuses on entry regulatory components that significantly contribute to economic and social growth. It also emphasises the importance of holding MNCs and development agencies legally accountable for their FDI impact on the environment.

Chapter 4 of this book is on regulating FDI for environmental development. It addresses the regulation of FDI-induced environmental issues in Bangladesh without delving into the debates between environmental and economic progress for long-term development.

Chapter 5 of this book covers the regulation of FDI for human rights protection, focusing on worker and employment rights, forced resettlements and private or Indigenous land rights against purchase or requisition for investment.

Chapter 6 delves into the legal arrangements and practices in Bangladesh for protecting national interests related to FDI, particularly expropriation and dispute resolution laws.

1.4 Significance of the Book

This book advances the legal understanding of FDI, especially in emerging and least developed countries. It offers fresh views and ideas for developing a sustainable FDI legal framework. Additionally, it advances trade, investment and commercial law understanding. The multidisciplinary approach of this study expands our knowledge of the environment, human rights and development economics and their effects on investment.

Practicality is as crucial as intellectual relevance in this text, if not more so. FDI strategists and policymakers in developing and least developed nations want liberalisation because they think FDI always leads to development. They see more rules as impediments to FDI in their country. This unique study challenges this common thinking and encourages the building of an ideal and development-oriented FDI legislative framework based on this information.

This book's practical significance is huge domestically and globally since it's about Bangladesh. It helps politicians, attorneys, executives and academics learn about FDI-led development rules nationwide. It also guides policymakers and lawmakers in FDI legal, institutional and policy changes to boost development. It may also spur economic, environmental and labour policy improvements.

This book may help state officials negotiate BITs abroad to further their national interests. This study may help other developing and least developed nations build their FDI regulatory regimes.

1.5 Concluding Remarks

The liberalised approach to the entry and operation of FDI alone is not sufficient to achieve the desired development goals in countries like Bangladesh and other developing and least developed nations. It is essential to simultaneously implement development-oriented regulations related to entry, fiscal and financial incentives and the protection of the environment and human rights. The FDI legal framework in Bangladesh is traditionally influenced by a liberalised approach, but it has not adequately addressed development issues. Therefore, this study proposes a detailed analysis of existing laws and policies relevant to FDI entry and operation in Bangladesh to evaluate their effectiveness, adequacy and suitability from a development perspective, with the ultimate goal of implementing reforms and changes aligned with the principles of sustainable development. This study will focus on broader issues related to major economic and social development areas that are potentially impacted by FDI operations, such as tax and financial regulations, as well as the protection of the environment and human rights. It aims to contribute to the development of scholarly literature in the field of foreign investment and policies and to provide guidance for the adoption of regulatory policies for FDI operations at the national level, filling the current gap in research in Bangladesh.

Notes

1 See M Sornaraja, *The International Law on Foreign Investment* (Cambridge University Press, 3rd ed., 2010) 53; see also, Sherif H Seid, *Global Regulation of Foreign Direct Investment* (Ashgate, 2002) 17–21.
2 M Sornaraja, *The International Law on Foreign Investment* (Cambridge University Press, 3rd ed., 2010) 53; see also, Sherif H Seid, *Global Regulation of Foreign Direct Investment* (Ashgate, 2002) 17–21.
3 M Sornaraja, *The International Law on Foreign Investment* (Cambridge University Press, 3rd ed., 2010) 48; Sherif H Seid, *Global Regulation of Foreign Direct Investment* (Ashgate, 2002) 14–15.
4 See Karl P Suvant, 'FDI Protectionism Is on the Rise' (Policy Research Working Paper No. 5052, The World Bank, 2009) <http://elibrary.worldbank.org/doi/book/10.1596/1813-9450-5052> 26 April 2024.
5 See UNCTAD, *World Investment Report 2001 Promoting Linkages* (2001) 6 <unctad.org/en/docs/ wir2001overview_en.pdf> 26 April 2024.
6 See UNCTAD, *World Investment Report 2005 Transnational Corporations and the Internationlisation of R&D* (2005) 22 <unctad.org/en/docs/wir2005overview_en.pdf> 20 December 2013.
7 Sornarajah, above n 1, 56.
8 It means that allowing big firms by FDI to compete with local firms can drive local firms out of business. See Yahya Z D Alhijazi, *Developing Countries and Foreign Direct Investment* (LL.M book, McGill University, 1999) 11.
9 For example, the gas leak incident from a pesticide plant of a subsidiary of the TNC Union Carbide in Bhopal, India, in 1984 that left more than 5,000 people dead, more than 500,000 injured, caused severe birth defects to more than 100,000 children, major economic hardship, massive environmental damage and economic misery beyond the realms of imagination; see V P Nanda, 'Export of Hazardous

Waste and Hazardous Technology: A Challenge of International Environmental Law'(1988) 17 *Denver Journal of International Law and Policy* 155, 165–70; the activities of McMoran in Indonesia leading to the violation of human rights and environmental damage; the activities of Royal Dutch Shell in Ogoniland, Nigeria, resulting in deaths, human suffering and destruction of the environment; S F Puvimansinghe, *Foreign Investment, Human Rights and the Environment: A Perspective from South Asia on the Role of Public International Law for Development* (Martinus Nijhoff Publishers, 2007) 1–3.

10 Sornaraja, above n 1, 56.

11 For example, Malaysia has instituted and maintained currency controls. Similar restrictive controls on investment can be seen in Africa, where Nigeria, Eritrea and the Central African Republic have increased controls on foreign investment. In Latin America, changes have been instituted by left-leaning governments. Widespread nationalization took place in the natural resources sector.

12 See M Sornarajah, above n 1, 55. The concept of a "middle path" is explained in Chapter 2 of this book.

13 L D Solomon and D H Mirsky, 'Direct Foreign Investment in the Caribbean: A Legal and Policy Analysis' (1990–91) 11 *North Western Journal of International Law and Business* 252, 259.

14 Sherif H Seid, *Global Regulation of Foreign Direct Investment* (Ashgate, 2002) 194.

2 Regulating FDI for Development

2.1 Introduction

Foreign direct investment (FDI) can benefit the economy and society. These include increasing capital, creating jobs, improving technology and management expertise, expanding the industrial sector and integrating into international markets by exporting more goods. Consequently, in recent years, there has been a more relaxed approach to regulating and overseeing FDI to attract more investment, especially in developing and least developed economies.

The liberalisation process in global governance is seen as a successful means of motivating and increasing investment flows. However, it's important to note that an increase in FDI flow cannot guarantee benefits for sustainable development unless it is properly regulated. Liberalisation of FDI has the potential to negatively impact the economic and social conditions of the host states. Unregulated operation of FDI by multinational corporations (MNCs) can create challenges for the host country's implementation of its development policies.

Elements of sustainable development, such as economic growth, environmental protection and social development, require effective legal and regulatory measures, just as with FDI. Regulation for FDI operation is essential for a host country that wants to optimise its positive benefits while addressing challenges and negative impacts. In support of this view, this chapter will first address the concept of FDI and its determinants, then explore the interrelation between development and regulation and finally suggest a development-oriented regulatory framework.

2.2 FDI Defined

FDI is an important aspect of the global economy. It is a well-known word that has received special attention from international financial institutions, researchers and international and national trade investment law and policymakers since the notion of economic globalisation emerged. Consequently, numerous definitions have been produced so far, and they seem identical in context. All definitional terminology revolves around one's investment in a

DOI: 10.4324/9781003469117-2

foreign country with some ownership control for the purpose of operating. Therefore, the author likes to argue that FDI is an "investment by a foreign person, corporate organisation, or financial institution in a nation other than its own, with precise ownership control to operate in targeted sectors". This definition is consistent with Moosa's view, which defines FDI as "the process by which residents of one country (the source country) acquire ownership of assets to control the production, distribution, and other activities of a firm in another country".[1] However, using the term "residents of one nation" to refer to the participants in the investment restricts the scope of this concept. Alternatively, the term "nationals of one country" might refer to all natural and juristic individuals residing in a country.

Sornarajah's concept of FDI is broader and more thorough in this regard. He defines foreign investment as the transfer of physical and intangible assets from one nation to another for use in that country to produce wealth under the owner's entire or partial control.[2] According to this definition, the transfer of physical or intangible property from one country to another by any actor, whether a person, a private or state-owned corporation or any agency, constitutes FDI. However, the investor, whether full or partial owner, should control the property's use.

The question of ownership interest and control is emphasised in multilateral financial institutions' definitions of FDI. The International Monetary Fund's (IMF) Balance of Payments Manual defines FDI as "an investment made to acquire a lasting interest in an enterprise operating in an economy other than that of the investor, with the investor's purpose being to have an effective voice in the management of the enterprise". The Organisation for Economic Co-operation and Development (OECD) and United Nations Conference on Trade and Development (UNCTAD) definitions place a premium on "long-term partnership" and long-term interest.[3] Long-term relationships and lasting interest indicate the nature of the investment; it should be made to establish and facilitate a continuing relationship between the investor and a direct investment enterprise in a foreign country and is associated with significant management influence over the latter.[4]

Financial institutions often use the two phrases mentioned to define FDI. These phrases distinguish FDI from portfolio investment because portfolio investment does not aim for control or long-term interest.[5] Portfolio investing separates corporate administration and control from ownership stake, while direct investment requires control over invested assets.[6] What precisely constitutes control is an unresolved question, although the frequently accepted minimum shareholding of 10 per cent is viewed as allowing a foreign corporation to have considerable influence over an underlying project's major policies. However, discussing how to achieve managerial control in a business is controversial, and discussing this topic seems inappropriate for this section.

Given the debate over the definition of FDI, two fundamental requirements must be met to qualify as FDI: (1) a transfer of capital from a source nation to a host country by a person or a corporation and (2) control via significant equity holdings. However, there is a gap between these two constituent pieces. The transfer of funds is not a strict criterion for an investment to be considered foreign. The contribution to the legal capital of a project or business by a foreign person or firm, a foreign government-owned company, an intergovernmental agency or a non-resident citizen of the host country is critical.

Considering the preceding debate on definition, it is reasonable to conclude that, as one of the most rapidly developing economic challenges, the definition of FDI is not static but rather fluid and progressive, frequently increasing wider and more inclusive. This trend is particularly seen in bilateral investment treaties and national law. Bilateral investment treaties (BITs) for capital-exporting tend to widen the definition area, bringing a wide range of investment-related activities within treaty protection. On the other hand, definitions in national law are heavily influenced by the states' national economic policies regarding the importance of FDI for economic growth.

2.3 Legal Regulation of FDI

It is widely recognised that legal regulation over all internal affairs occurring in a country's territorial jurisdiction is a county's inherent right. From this point of view, a host state can exert its control over FDI through laws and policies at the entry and operational stages. As a concept of cross-border capital movement, FDI involves economic activities by an alien in a foreign state that concerns some legal issues intended for the promotion, control and protection of investment and the protection of the investors. The country hosting FDI has to ensure legal protection to the investment property and investors, as well as a corresponding right to regulate them as needed to meet its intended development goals from FDI. The importance of the legal regulation of FDI within a national territory increased largely after the post-colonial era due to the emergence of independent states as a claim of sovereign rights.

The right of a state to regulate is based upon the notion of "state sovereignty" within its territorial jurisdiction. The sovereign right to regulate the activity of foreign investment is recognised by both international and national law instruments. It is also firmly established in customary international law, as an attribute of state sovereignty.[7] *The UN Charter of Economic Rights and Duties of States 1974* establishes the principle of a state's permanent sovereignty over all of the natural resources, economic activities and wealth within its territory.[8] The principle of permanent sovereignty recognises "...the right of a host State to regulate and exercise authority over, and supervise the activities of, foreign investors in accordance with laws and regulations and conformity with its national objectives and social priorities".[9] In the course of this, a state also has the right to regulate and supervise the activities of transnational corporations (TNCs) or MNCs, the main actors of FDI operating in its jurisdiction, and requires their activities to comply with national laws and regulations.

The state's sovereign right to regulate FDI is also confirmed by the *UN Resolution 1803 on Permanent Sovereignty over Natural Resources 1962*. The Resolution provides the framework of principles and rules conferring the right upon the states to regulate the operations of FDI for the exploration, development and disposition of natural resources. The principles and rules governing authorisation, restrictions or prohibitions of economic activities regarding natural resources must conform with national laws and conditions set freely by the people and states concerned based on needs and interests.[10]

The *Calvo doctrine*[11] recognises sovereignty as paramount, which indicates that a state may enjoy the right to regulate the economic activities of alien investors. Although the concept of absolute sovereignty, as perceived by the *Calvo doctrine*, is the subject of immense criticism in the face of the growing concept of economic cooperation led by supra-national institutions, this does not militate against the state's right of regulation for its developmental need.

Given the perceived right to regulation as established under international law, host states are justified in exercising control over FDI following their national laws and policies to foster economic and social progress for their people's benefit. The regulation does not necessitate curtailing or affecting the investors' fundamental rights to protect their properties and persons in line with established international standards. Moreover, the right to regulation can be qualified through treaty commitments or general international law rules regarding the treatment of aliens.

FDI regulation entails imposing entry restrictions and operational requirements to ensure investments are consistent with the host state's economic laws and policies. Through entry restrictions, a state can ensure that FDI suits its development objectives and interests. For instance, a host can impose conditions for investment in a particular region, require certain types of direct investment such as joint ventures with local partners, forbid investment in certain sectors, impose a minimum local equity restriction or environmental certification, etc.[12] Entry control can be exercised by imposing screening, licensing requirements and several approvals or administrative clearances by the host states' central or local authorities. A state can exclude foreign investment if the conditions are not satisfied.

The imposition of conditions upon the entry of investment or exclusion is based on the accepted rule that the host state laws would control the whole process as it is the prerogative power of the sovereign state. The law of the host state could specify the provisions through which the foreign investment should be made, the nature of capital resources that should be brought from outside the state, the planning and environmental controls that manufacturing plants should be subject to and the required circumstances of the termination of foreign investment and other similar matters.[13]

The law of the host state can also specify the operational regulations of FDI, which might include local content requirements, technology transfer requirements, economic and fiscal regulation (foreign exchange and remittance restriction, product licensing, export performance requirements), local employment restrictions, environmental regulation and, above all, regulation related to the protection of human rights. All these regulatory issues are mainly based on a country's national development and eco-politico security interests.

Legal approaches to regulating foreign investments vary widely based on domestic political considerations, economic theories, development objectives and perceived national interests. The trend of introducing entry and operational regulation given development objectives is rare in the specific laws for FDI in developing host countries. However, in developed countries, there are legislations and regulations dealing with different entry and operational conditions that exclude FDI on the grounds of national interest and development.

For instance, the *Foreign Acquisitions and Takeovers Act of 1975* in Australia states that the Government must determine whether proposed foreign acquisitions are consistent with Australia's national interest. Australia even announced a new policy in 2008 for proposed investment by sovereign investors. It requires the reviews of applications by investors, taking into consideration six issues that determine whether an investor's operations are independent of relevant foreign government, the investor's observance of standards of business behaviour, the investment's impact on Australia's national security and the contribution of an investment to the country's economy and community.[14] Likewise, Japan's *Foreign Exchange and Foreign Trade Act* declares that foreign investments that are likely to impair national security, disturb the maintenance of public order, hinder the protection of public safety or have a significant adverse effect on the "smooth management of the Japanese economy" must be screened by the Ministry of Finance. The review of these examples reveals that the state deserves the right of regulation or control over the entry and establishment of FDI to the extent necessary for or consistent with development goals and public interests.

2.4 General Forms of FDI Regulation

The issues of FDI can be regulated in three ways: unilateral, bilateral and multilateral. Unilateral regulation is the first form of regulation that refers to the national laws of a host country that regulate FDI. These regulations cover a wide range of laws; they include specific laws enacted for regulating FDI as well as any domestic law that governs the post-entry operation of corporations engaging in FDI, such as tax law, laws relating to currency regulation, labour and employment law, property law, corporate law, environmental law and laws relating to mining or exploitation of natural resources. All these laws represent a country's policy and regulatory character towards FDI. Unilateral regulation can also be established by national policy directives in different respects.

The second form of regulation is bilateral regulation, which usually takes the form of a BIT, which is an agreement between capital exporting and importing countries regulating the investment between them.[15] BITs originated from the earliest treaties known as treaties of friendship, commerce and navigation, which have become more investment-specific since the beginning of the 1960s and thus provided rules for international investments by corporations.[16] BITs have developed to provide a certain level of stability and also as an effort to safeguard foreign investments in host countries.

The regulatory issues under BITs are determined by the bilateral negotiations between home and host countries; hence, the terms and conditions of BITs applying to investment vary depending on the position of the contracting parties in each BIT. As a result, each BIT creates country-specific obligations instead of creating any law at an international level.[17] BITs contain clauses that require parties to keep commitments made to each other's nationals. Therefore, the obligation created by BITs extends to the nationals and corporates of the contracting parties. BITs govern international investment activities in addition to the national investment laws and regulations and thus complement and supplement the national FDI laws.

Investment agreements between host states and any entity of BIT contracting parties are also treated as regulatory elements in relation to their commercial aspects. Examples include concession agreements, product sharing agreements, management agreements, licensing agreements and transfer of technology agreements. These agreements are usually guided by the BIT provisions in the legal treatment and investment protection.[18]

Multilateral regulation refers to a framework consisting of international rules and regulations driven by international instruments such as WTO rules, regulations related to investment, regional free trade agreements (FTAs), international codes of conduct and guidelines for TNCs. A review of the relevant international instruments reveals no comprehensive international investment regulation in today's world. The OECD took the initiative to conclude a multilateral investment agreement, which failed to materialise due to protests from developing countries and NGOs. They argued that the MAI did not adequately consider the protection of the environment and other social concerns, such as human rights and labour standards, which MNCs are capable of disregarding.

The World Trade Organization (WTO) regime under Trade-Related Investment Measures (TRIMs), General Agreement on Trade in Services (GATS) and Trade-Related Aspects of Intellectual Properties (TRIPS) partially covers some issues of FDI without creating any specific obligation for multinational enterprises (MNEs) or MNCs in their operations. They are mainly meant to facilitate trade-related and non-trade investment issues by lifting restrictions and providing protection. Similarly, although the corporate codes of conduct provide some directive principles as regards the responsibility of MNEs or MNCs for environmental management and human rights treatment, they are soft and do not have the status of binding regulation. Therefore, MNEs or MNCs are mainly subject to the national laws of the home country, where they are established as accepted international law principles.

There are certain circumstances where MNCs encounter difficulties and conflicts in their treatment, and these relate to FDI implications for the economic, environmental and social development of a host country. The problems range from double taxation, repatriation of profit, compensation, employment by MNCs, operation of MNCs involving environmental protection and promotion of general principles of human rights, labour and employment relations, technology transfer and overall MNCs responsibilities to the group rights of citizens of the host country.

Therefore, there is a need for some common standards and guidelines for regulating investor firms' behaviour and responsibilities in these issues at the international level. However, a lack of an international standard or agreed-upon set of rules and regulations still exists due to the absence of multilateral treaty frameworks for FDI. Against this backdrop, the solution to problems must be sought using a rule-based approach under unilateral and bilateral regulation, as these are the main ways to regulate FDI.

However, the current unilateral legal regimes for FDI, especially in developing and least developed countries, are little concerned with the abovementioned development issues; they mostly tend to the liberalisation of FDI to win the ongoing competition for FDI inflows. The specific legislations for FDI, therefore, in most cases, focus only on the promotion and protection of investment, such as provisions relating to expropriation, compensation, repatriation and other fiscal or financial incentives. On the other hand, the provisions of relevant laws such as company, labour, environment and property lack specificity and certainty in relation to foreign investment operations.

The BITs are similarly formulated using the liberalisation approach in relation to entry and post-entry–post-operations with a strong commitment to investment protection. Because of this, BITs between developed and developing host countries, in many cases, seem to be nothing but a single-minded and investor-biased instrument, although some changes have taken place in recent years to match the development demands of developing economies. Under this situation, the application of national laws and BITs is seen as more conducive to serving the interests of investors rather than the development objectives of the host countries. Therefore, to make the aims and objectives of FDI meaningful in the context of the host country, the legal framework, whether national or bilateral, needs to be balanced, that is, less pro-investors and more development-oriented.

2.5 Concluding Remarks

The ongoing trend to regulate the FDI operation in a country is more often double-facet, meaning through national laws as well as adopting bilateral agreements between host and home states of investors. Both national laws and bilateral treaties consider entry regulation, internal protection of investment properties, internal revenues earning, profit repatriation and dispute settlement. In regulating the FDI operations, the host country enjoys the right to determine the regulation approach. As location choice is a vital issue for foreign investors, the current trend is that the host countries adopt a liberalisation approach through law and policymaking to encourage investors. Although the instrumentality of liberalisation appears to be logical for achieving the purpose of investment growth and the increase in revenue earning, it often turns more investor-interest-biased when especially the investors are from northern economies and thus creates potential failure to contribute to the host state's development agenda. So, the holistic consideration of development necessitates an optimum balance between liberalisation and strict regulation.

Notes

1 Imad A Moosa, *Foreign Direct Investment: Theory, Evidence and Practice* (Palgrave Macmillan, 2002) 1.
2 M Sornarajah, *The International Law on Foreign Investment* (Cambridge, 3rd ed., 2010) 8.
3 See also OECD, *OECD Benchmark Definition of Foreign Direct Investment* (4th ed., 1996) <http://www.oecd.org> 26 April 2024.
4 See Maitena Duce and Banco de Espana, *Definitions of Foreign Direct Investment (FDI): A Methodological Note* (final draft, 2003), Economics and International Relations Department, Bank for International Settlements <www.bis.org/publ/cgfs22bde3.pdf> 26 April 2024; see also OECD, *OECD Benchmark Definition of Foreign Direct Investment* (4th ed., 1996) <http://www.oecd.org> 26 April 2024.
5 Moosa, above n 1, 1.
6 Sornarajah, above n 2, 8. According to Sornarajah, such a distinction is drawn in the texts on economics and is also a sound basis for distinguishing direct and portfolio investment in the law.
7 Ibrahim FI Shihata, 'Regulation of Foreign Investment' (2004) 2 *International Sustainable Development Law* <http://www.eolss.net/Sample-Chapters/C13/E6-67-03-04.pdf> 26 April 2024.
8 *The UN Charter of Economic Rights and Duties (1974)* art. 2 (1) (2); see also Subrata Roy Chowdhury, 'Permanent Sovereignty over Natural Resources: Substratum of the Seoul Declaration' in Paul De Waart et al. (eds) *International Law and Development* (Martinus Nijhoff, 1988) 59, 59; Emeka Duruigbo, 'Permanent Sovereignty and People's Ownership of Natural Resources in International Law' (2006) 38 *George Washington International Law Review* 33, 38.
9 *The UN Charter of Economic Rights and Duties (1974)* art. 2 (1) (2); see also Subrata Roy Chowdhury, 'Permanent Sovereignty over Natural Resources: Substratum of the Seoul Declaration' in Paul De Waart et al. (eds) *International Law and Development* (Martinus Nijhoff, 1988) 59, 59; Emeka Duruigbo, 'Permanent Sovereignty and People's Ownership of Natural Resources in International Law' (2006) 38 *George Washington International Law Review* 33, 38.
10 *The UN Charter of Economic Rights and Duties (1974)* art. 2 (1) (2); see also Subrata Roy Chowdhury, 'Permanent Sovereignty over Natural Resources: Substratum of the Seoul Declaration' in Paul De Waart et al. (eds) *International Law and Development* (Martinus Nijhoff, 1988) 59, 59; Emeka Duruigbo, 'Permanent

Sovereignty and People's Ownership of Natural Resources in International Law' (2006) 38 *George Washington International Law Review* 33, 38.

11 The Clavo Doctrine is the body of international rules regulating the jurisdiction of the governments over aliens. The doctrine was advanced by the Argentine diplomat and legal scholar Carlos Calvo in his "International Law of Europe and America in Theory and Practice" (1868).

12 See *Canada v Cain* (1906) AC 542, 546. It was observed by the Privy Council that one of the rights possessed by the supreme power in every state is the right to refuse the alien to enter that state, to annex what conditions it pleases to the permission to enter it and to expel or to depart from the state. See also *Schmidt v Secretary for Home Affairs* (1969) 2 Ch 149, 168, where Lord Denning said: "At common law, no alien has any right to enter this country except by the leave of the Crown; and the Crown can refuse to leave without giving any reason". The common law has been modified by the statute.

13 Sornarajah, above n 2, 90.

14 The Department of the Treasury, Australia, 'Government Improves Transparency of Foreign Investment Screening Process' (Media Release, No. 009, 17 February 2008) <http://ministers.treasury.gov.au/DisplayDocs.aspx?doc=pressreleases/2008/009.htm&pageID=003&min=wms&Year=&DocType> 26 April 2024.

15 There are two different objectives pursued by capital-exporting states and host countries in BITs. The creation of clear rules and effective enforcement mechanisms to protect investment are the primary objectives of capital-exporting countries. The secondary objective is to facilitate the entry of their investment. The goals of host countries, on the other hand, are to encourage foreign capital flow to their territories and retain control over the entry and operation of FDI. S Salem-Haghighi, *MAI and BITs: A Comparative Study* (Research Paper, Institute of Comparative Law, Montreal, 1998) <www.comparativelaw. info/library.htm> 26 April 2024.

16 See Sornarajah, above n 2, 180.

17 See Sornarajah, above n 2, 180.

18 See Bernard Kishiyain, 'The Utility of Bilateral Investment Treaties in the Formulation of Customary International Law' (1993) 14 *Northwestern Journal of International Law and Business* 327, 328; see also Surya P Subedi, International Investment Law: Reconciling Policy and Principle (Hart Publishing, 2008) 84.

3 Entry Regulation of FDI

3.1 Introduction

When foreign investors seek to invest in a new country, they must comply with legal and administrative regulations to gain approval for their investment proposals. If these requirements are not met, they risk being excluded from the host state. The primary purpose of these regulations is to control foreign investment, and the specific objectives behind them can vary greatly depending on the country. National security, economic and developmental reasons and other factors may all influence the decision to restrict foreign investment.[1]

Generally, host countries evaluate proposals for foreign investment using two types of tests. Firstly, they consider whether the investment aligns with their national interests and would not harm their economies. Secondly, they evaluate whether the proposal aligns with their national economic and development policies. However, the definition of national interest is subjective and may differ from country to country.[2] In Australia, for example, they use a case-by-case screening regime based on a 'national interest' test,[3] which covers both economic and non-economic policy concerns.[4]

Host countries can impose restrictions on foreign investment in several ways, including capitalisation requirements, carve-outs/exclusions and ownership control.[5] Additionally, foreign direct investment (FDI) laws and policies may involve performance requirements, quantitative restrictions on foreign companies in specific sectors, environmental and export requirements, and screening or authorisation processes for investment proposals or designated industrial projects. These regulations are not intended to act as barriers to foreign entrepreneurship but rather to ensure that the developmental aspect of FDI is achieved on a case-by-case basis.[6]

It is worth noting that the absolute ban on FDI no longer exists, and contemporary FDI laws are trending towards liberalisation. The restrictions on entry are in place to provide control over foreign investment and to ensure that any potential investment aligns with the host country's national interests and economic and development policies. This is because foreign investment can positively and negatively affect a host country's economy, and it is important

DOI: 10.4324/9781003469117-3

to ensure that any potential investment aligns with the host country's goals and objectives. Overall, foreign investment regulations are intended to balance the benefits of foreign investment and the need to protect the interests of the host country.

3.2 Laws and Policies for Regulating the Entry of FDI in Bangladesh

The core legislation of FDI in Bangladesh – the Foreign Private Investment (Promotion and Protection) Act (FPIA) 1980 – does not provide specific rules focusing on legal or administrative requirements for admission of foreign investment. However, section 3 (1) of this law reflects on some directives to be considered by the authority while granting any foreign industrial undertaking. According to the section, in granting any establishment with foreign capital, a government may take into specific consideration the following matters:

1 If such establishment of industrial undertaking does not exist, how far is it desirable?
2 If it exists, is it being carried out on a scale adequate to socio-economic needs?
3 Whether this establishment of industrial undertaking is likely to contribute to:

   a the development of capital, technical and managerial resources of Bangladesh; or
   b the discovery, mobilisation or better utilisation of the natural resources; or
   c the strengthening of the balance of payment of Bangladesh; or
   d increasing employment opportunities in Bangladesh; or
   e the economic development of the country can be done in any other manner.

Subsection 3 (2) further states that the sanction of foreign investment may be subject to any condition the government thinks appropriate. The words under section 3 of the Act appear to be very indicative and focused on the consideration of development-oriented aspects of FDI at the event of entry. This includes consideration of the potential of FDI for developing capital, technical and managerial resources, exploration and better utilisation of natural resources, strengthening employment opportunities and, above all, economic development.

More importantly, the first consideration, as revealed by the wording (to test the desirability of an industrial undertaking in the event none of its kind is available), is very much encompassing. It may be considered from economic, social and cultural perspectives. Thus, it is easily drawn from the wording above that the law has mandated the government to impose any condition in conformity with the socio-economic development of the country itself at its discretion. The words of the section do not seem to be obligation-creating; rather, they can be used as a guideline for setting lenses for approving foreign investment for achieving said development purposes.

When approving an FDI proposal to achieve development goals, Bangladesh, as a host country, considers two types of entry regulatory aspects. The first type of regulation is commonly applied regardless of its relation to the operational impacts of FDI. The need for these regulations depends on the specific circumstances of the host state. They are mainly the following three:

1 Capitalisation requirement
2 Carving out or exclusion-related matters
3 Ownership restriction

There are various types of entry regulations, and one of them is operational regulations. These regulations are crucial for host countries to incorporate into their legal and policy frameworks, regardless of their situation. This helps achieve the development goals of FDI. Operational regulations include performance requirements, environment-related regulations and procedural screening.

3.3 Requirement of Screening of Investment Proposals

Screening has traditionally been very common and one of the main tools for controlling the access of FDI into a host country. It is a method of scrutiny that the host states apply, following their laws and policies, to decide on approving or rejecting foreign investment proposals. Foreign investors are often required to obtain certain approvals or permits before initiating business operations, and projects are screened to ensure that they conform to the established criteria.[7] There may be certain objectives to applying screening procedures as determined by the capital-importing country itself.[8] But the fundamental objective of screening is to examine or evaluate the foreign investment proposals as to whether or how far they suit the economic goals as defined by the host state's law and policies and what the potential impact of investment on the local economy; additionally, whether they have followed the established guidelines for investment in any specific type or form or any specified sector. It is well-indicated in the Armenian Code, as it states that certain economic activities '... may only be conducted by enterprises with foreign investment only after obtaining a license in the established manner'.[9]

There exists a division of opinions between international law writers about the general wisdom of such screening procedures. In the early stages, institutional writers such as Victoria and Vattle advocated the exercise of complete freedom of entry for trade and investment. Victoria believed in 'fundamental human rights, which requires all men to trade with the people of other lands and thus fulfills the human urge to the community'.[10] Several commentators consider the imposition of conditions such as screening as a major obstacle to foreign investment in developing countries.[11] However, such regulations are not uncommon where certain investments are considered to be opposed to national interests.[12]

In reality, screening regulations have been relaxed and simplified in different countries to a considerable extent compared to the post-liberalised communist era. The host countries mostly pursue an 'open door policy' requiring simple registration or prior authorisation for investment in several sectors. However, some developed and developing countries have resorted to or stuck to protective measures after the recent global economic recession. These include France, Australia, Canada, Japan, China, Russia and India. The screening system they have adopted varies, but they mostly involve the sectors that are economically sensitive and strategically important for national security purposes.[13]

Bangladesh pursues very relaxed policies to allow foreign investments, which are mainly confined to a mere registration process after completing incorporation procedures under the existing company laws. There is no policy guideline adopted by the Bangladesh Development Agency (formerly Board of Investment, in short called BoI), the main approving or registering authority in Bangladesh, consistent with directives of section 3 of the Act 1980, as discussed earlier. However, it maintains a certain administrative procedure requirement for registering a new foreign project.

The registration or approval process is different based on the nature of the investment projects. For joint ventures or 100 per cent foreign equity investment projects, there is no requirement for prior approval or a no-objection certificate (NOC) to set up units. However, these investments must be registered with Bangladesh Investment Development Authority (BIDA) to take advantage of various financial and fiscal incentives, facilities and institutional support. Registration with BIDA is also necessary to obtain benefits such as importing machinery at concessionary duty rates or importing items on the 'restricted list'. However, pre-registration clearance is a requirement for investment in RMGs, banks, insurance companies and other financial institutions.

For private investment, either foreign or local, the industries are categorised into three groups: thrust sectors, reserved sectors and controlled sectors.[14] According to the National Industrial Policy (NIP) 2010, investment in the controlled sector cannot be registered with Bangladesh Investment Development Authority (BIDA) or Bangladesh Economic Zones Authority (BEZA) (formerly Bangladesh Export Processing Zones Authority [BEPZA]) unless approval or NOC is obtained from the Ministry of Industry and Commerce or the concerned ministry or commission, as discussed earlier. The government can fix the equity rate of local foreign investors for any joint venture project in this sector.

A separate condition applies to the registration of joint venture enterprises with BIDA. If a local or foreign entrepreneur wishes to set up a joint venture with a public sector corporation, it must be registered with BIDA if the private sector's equity participation is more than 50 per cent. In such a case it is treated as a private sector project. The public sector entity in question must get approval from the concerned ministry to invest its resources, and the ministry then processes the registration.

BIDA is the main registering authority for private investment, be it local or foreign. But if a foreign enterprise is to be set up in an EPZ or industrial estate, the registration must take place with BEZA. For a manufacturing company employing ten or more workers, registration must also be done with the Chief Inspectors of Factories and Establishment under the *Bangladesh Labour Act* 2006 (BLA).[15] This requirement is intended to regulate the working conditions and ensure industry safety measures.

BIDA is a one-stop service provider that usually provides quick service to applicants for registration. In addition, it also helps get environmental clearance certificates from the Department of Environment (DoE), as mentioned in the former section. The normal procedures for registration with BIDA are not cumbersome or time-consuming. The applicants are required to attach to the prescribed application form the following documents duly completed[16]:

1 Certificate of incorporation (including Memorandum and Articles of Association in case of a Public or Private Limited Company)
2 In the case of a Joint Venture Project (JVP), a JVP Agreement (signed by both parties)
3 Deeds/documents in support of project land (either purchase deeds or in the case of lease and rental premises, a deed of agreement)
4 Total estimated cost of the project (if the total cost exceeds Taka 50 million, the submission of a project profile is necessary)
5 Personal details of the investors (permanent and mailing address, nationality and position)
6 List of machinery (with the indication of quantity and price) and the supporting documents of loan (if the project is financed by loan)

After receiving the application duly submitted in association with aforesaid required documents, BIDA reviews and, if found suitable, issues the registration certificate within seven days. Although BIDA is supposed to complete the required processes quickly, some investors report difficulty obtaining registration due to bureaucratic red tape and administrative corruption.

Apart from BIDA, for industries to be registered under BEZA, the investor must apply in the prescribed form. Upon receipt of the application, the authority or any person authorised to act on this behalf shall grant him permission in the prescribed form if he finds that the investor satisfies all of the requirements for setting up an industry in the zone.[17] The requirements are not specifically set under any policy; they are determined by the guidelines the government provides from time to time. However, at least the NIP 2010 settles that only export-oriented industries can be set up in the EPZ. To be export-oriented, the industry is required to export at least 80 per cent of its produce or supply 80 per cent of its output as raw materials for exportable items. The same requirement applies to service enterprises.

3.4 Concluding Remarks

The entire discussion reflects an inconsistency between the directives introduced in section 3 of FPIA 1980 and the legal and policy initiatives regarding entry regulation for development purposes. The review of overall entry regulatory aspects reveals a lack of concern from the state for the exigency of introducing such issues in laws, policies or treaty negotiations, while the concept of FDI-induced development gains in currency and influences progress in other host states' laws and policies. The laws and policies in Bangladesh are still influenced by the liberalised and permissive attitude to admitting FDI. No legal changes have accommodated the entry regulatory issue since the legal regime emerged in 1980. In addition, no screening manual is reportedly adopted by BoI consistent with the directives of section 3 or general regulatory aspects mentioned above that may enable Bangladesh to reap any FDI-driven development benefit. The industrial division based on regulation in the NIP is a good initiative, but for its due enforcement and application, there needs to be some concrete, specific legal provisions. Procedural restriction alone is not sufficient.

There is plenty of scope for legal and policy reforms regarding entry regulation. Firstly, there should be an amendment in the text of section 3 to give it the status of a legally binding force. Therefore, the word 'may' needs to be replaced by 'shall' to denote obligatory expression. As the performance requirement is very much cardinal for realising the development objective of FDI, there should be legal principles requiring conditional performance requirements for authorisation or the gaining of incentives. Secondly, a screening manual must focus on the entry regulatory aspects in line with the directives of section 3 of FPIA 1980. Thirdly, some legal provisions need to be added to FPIA 1980 regarding forms of investment, defining their nature, scope and application conditions. Fourthly, in the case of joint ventures or fully owned foreign investments, there needs to be some policy reform regarding capital contribution and local content requirements under NIP. Moreover, the requirement for technology transfer can be imposed in joint venture investments. Finally, a ministerial committee under the auspices of BoI can be formed for official screening.

Notes

1 M. Sornaraja, *The International Law on Foreign Investment* (Cambridge University Press, 3rd ed., 2010) 53; Simon Reich, 'Roads to Follow: Regulating Foreign Direct Investment' (1989) 43 (4) *International Organization* 543.
2 *The Foreign Acquisition and Takeovers Act* 1975 (Australia) art. 25 (1A).
3 Vivienne Bath, 'Foreign Investment, the National Interest and National Security – Foreign Direct Investment in Australia and China' (2012) 34 (1) *The Sydney Law Review*, 5, 5.
4 Andrew Lumsden, *The National Interest Test and Australian Foreign Investment Laws* (2007) Centre for Law, Markets & Regulations UNSW<http://www.clmr.unsw.edu.au/article/accountability/national-interest-test-australia> 26 April 2024.
5 Sherif H Seid, *Global Regulation of Foreign Direct Investment* (Ashgate, 2002) 36.
6 Sherif H Seid, *Global Regulation of Foreign Direct Investment* (Ashgate, 2002) 36.
7 See UNIDO, *Guidelines for Foreign Investment Promotion Agencies* (2003) <http://www.unido.org> 26 April 2024.
8 Abdullah Al-yagout, *The Regulation of Foreign Investment in Kuwait: The Role of Law, Politics and Economics Policies in the Development Process* (PhD book at the University of Warwick, 1997) 142 <http://go.warwick.ac.uk/wrap> 26 April 2024.
9 *Law of the Republic of Armenia on Foreign Investments 1994* (Armenia) Article 14.
10 Abdullah Al-yagout, *The Regulation of Foreign Investment in Kuwait: The Role of Law, Politics and Economics Policies in the Development Process* (PhD book at the University of Warwick, 1997) 142 <http://go.warwick.ac.uk/wrap> 26 April 2024.
11 A A Fatouros, *Government Guarantees to Foreign Direct Investment* (Columbia University Press, 1962) 290; see UNCTAD, *The Development Dimension of FDI: Policy and Rule Making Perspectives* (2003) <unctad.org/en/Docs/iteiia20034_en.pdf> 26 April 2024.
12 Shahita comments on the screening position that all or most proposed investments are subject to scrutiny or screening by the authorities and must receive a formal approval, such as an investment licence, before an investment can actually be made. Pursuant to these provisions, the screening process typically involves an assessment of the projected investment's economic impact and, in particular, of the economic benefits that may accrue to the host country from investment. For more about admission under national legislation, see Ibrahim Shahita, 'Recent Trends Relating to Entry of Foreign Direct Investment' in Heng et al. (eds.) *Current Legal Issues in Internationalization of Business Enterprises* (Butterworth, 1996).
13 For example, in Australia, under the *Foreign Acquisitions and Takeovers Act of 1975*, the Government must determine whether proposed foreign acquisitions are consistent with Australia's national interest. A new policy was announced in February 2008 for proposed investments by sovereign investors. It requires the review of applications to consider six specific issues, including whether an investor's operations are independent of the relevant foreign government, the investor's observance of the standard of business behaviour, the investment's impact on national security and the contribution of an investment to the country's economy and community. In Japan, according to its *Foreign Exchange and Foreign Trade Act*, foreign investment that potentially impairs national security, disturbs the maintenance of public order, hinders the protection of public safety or has a significant adverse effect on the smooth management of the Japanese economy must be screened by the Ministry of Finance and the Ministry having jurisdiction over the business. China strengthened its review system in August 2006 by announcing the *Provisions on Merger and Acquisition of Domestic Enterprises by Foreign Investors*. Under this,

a new screening mechanism was developed, which was further enhanced in a five-year plan of National Development adopted in November of the same year. Besides this, it also enacted an anti-monopoly law in August 2008. In Russia, a 2008 law on *Procedures for Foreign Investments in Companies of Strategic Importance of National Defense and Security* requires government approval for certain transactions involving foreign investors if (i) the Russian company is engaged in an activity of strategic importance to the country's defence and national security and (ii) the foreign investor would control either the company or rights to 'natural resource deposits having federal importance'. For more, see Karl P Sauvant, *FDI Protectionism Is on the Rise* (Policy Research Working Paper No. 5052, World Bank, September 2009) <www.worldbank.org> or <www.vcc.columbia.edu> 27 April 2024.

14 Thrust sectors include 32 industrial sectors that currently occupy a dominant position in the economy or have high growth potentials but are currently non-existent or nascent. The government may extend the number of the sectors from time to time in consultation with all stakeholders and based on information collected on various industries, their growth potentials and likely positive impact on the economy (Chapter 3 and annexure 11 of NIP 2010). There are four reserved areas, which are exclusively limited to public investment (Chapter 3 and Annexure 3 of NIP 2010). Controlled sectors include 17 industrial sectors that might have a negative impact on the economy or cause a threat to national security and culture (Chapter 3 and Annexure 4 of NIP 2010).

15 It was previously under the *Factories Act, 1965*, which was annulled and its provisions were merged with the newly adopted *Bangladesh Labour Act, 2010*.

16 See Board of Investment, Bangladesh, *Investing in Bangladesh (Handbook & Guidelines, 2011)* <www.boi.gov.bd> 27 April 2024; see also *The Board of Investment Act of 1989* (Bangladesh) s. 11.

17 *The Bangladesh Export Processing Zones Authority Act 1980* (Bangladesh) s. 12.

4 FDI and Environmental Protection

4.1 Introduction

The environmental impact of foreign direct investment (FDI) is a significant concern in host countries today. As the use of FDI increases, transnational corporations (TNCs) play an increasingly pivotal role in economic activities, drawing attention to the resulting environmental implications.[1] Recent catastrophic incidents have raised concerns about the performance of TNCs in developing host countries, often viewed as "pollution havens".[2] Efforts are being made at the international level to set standards for the environmental responsibilities of TNCs. These efforts are influencing the development of laws and regulations in host countries as they aim to regulate TNCs' activities to protect the environment and promote their development goals.

The international environmental standards for the operation of TNCs are primarily developed by the Organization for Economic Co-operation and Development (OECD) Guidelines and Agenda 21.[3] The provisions under these instruments are non-binding and merely directive in nature. An initiative was also taken under the Multilateral Investment Agreement (MAI), but it failed to receive the required ratifications due to a north-south conflict of interests. However, this issue has increasingly become a reference in International Investment Agreements (IIAs), and as a result, a regulatory regime for the environmental conduct of foreign multinationals is now emerging based on mutual cooperation and cross-border management systems. In response to international environmental regulations, many developing countries are establishing statutory standards. There is a growing emphasis on pre-entry environmental requirements and the development of a regulatory framework for post-entry operations. The environmental issue has also been gaining prominence in recent FDI legislation as a special policy agenda. However, national environmental laws and regulations, which are applied equally to local and foreign enterprises, continue to be the primary means of addressing environmental concerns. Moreover, some country-specific laws have adopted guidelines for regulating FDI-linked pollution-intensive industries and sensitive investment activities, such as infrastructural development and natural resource extraction.[4]

DOI: 10.4324/9781003469117-4

Foreign multinationals have operated in Bangladesh for the last four decades as a source of FDI investments. The investments range over most industrial sectors, including some more environmentally risky and pollution-intensive sectors such as infrastructure, energy, minerals and marine resources. Their activities certainly have implications for the country's environment. Some recent incidents have contributed to increased concern for the environmental performance of multinationals. The recent *Tengratila* and *Magur Chara* blowout incidents caused by the Canadian company Niko and the US Company Unocal, respectively, are striking examples.[5]

Bangladesh is recognised as one of the most environmentally precarious countries, with corporate activities significantly contributing to land-based and river pollution and deforestation. Since gaining independence, Bangladesh has implemented various laws, policies and institutional mechanisms to address industrial pollution control and management. These include the National Environmental Policy 1992, the Environmental Conservation Act (ECA) 1995, the Environmental Conservation Rules (ECR) 1997 (now replaced by subsequent rules) and the Environment Conservation Rules 2023. The country has a dedicated ministry for the environment, under which the Department of Environment (DoE) is responsible for enforcing environmental regulations and protection through implementing laws and rules. Although FDI-related environmental issues are not specifically addressed in these laws and policies, FDI operations are subject to these regulations.

4.2 FDI-Related Law and Policy for Protecting the Environment in Bangladesh

The legislation enacted in 1980 to promote FDI in Bangladesh does not provide any provision for creating responsibility for investors to ensure environmental protection in their performance. There has been no further amendment of this text to date to address any emerging global concern, such as the environment or human rights, or to cater to the current developmental need. This law is mainly intended to stimulate investors by offering a combined approach of incentives and protection for investment, where the duties and obligations of investors are absent entirely. Therefore, it includes some very traditional and common contents of the FDI legal regime as contained in most of the FDI-related laws of developing host states, such as the principles of fair and equitable treatment, safeguarding foreign investment from expropriation and nationalisation and assuring repatriation of finance and profit. It can be argued that it is not essential that environmental issues be integrated into the original text of investment law, as the environmental issues of foreign investment are automatically the subject of existing national environmental law principles and regulations. However, the advantage of mainstreaming the environmental issue into the legal framework is that the investment law would be more predictable by the investors, more specific and also more comprehensive. The textual specificity of any legal provision is very important for its due application and enforcement.

This issue, however, can be introduced in the policy framework or the admission and approval process designed for foreign investors by authorised governmental agencies. For example, in 1995, China promulgated two official documents regulating FDI. They are *Interim Provisions on Guiding Foreign Investment Direction* and the *Guiding List of Industries for Foreign Investors*.[6] Under these two official documents, FDI projects are divided into four categories based on economic and social prospects and priorities. One category is a prohibited category that covers projects likely to jeopardise national security, adversely affect social and public interests, pollute the environment, destroy natural resources or impair human health.[7] These documents also guide policy-implementing agencies in screening FDI with a view to maximising its benefits to the development process and minimising its negative effects with special reference to the environment. Furthermore, it has also promoted a post-approval screening and monitoring system, including adopting a mechanism of joint annual inspection and audit of foreign investment enterprises to ensure that TNC operations align with the host country's laws and regulations.[8] In addition, the *Regulation for the Implementation of the Chinese-Foreign Equity Joint Venture* stipulates that projects with a negative environmental impact should not be approved.[9]

In Bangladesh, there is still no public document specifying the issue relating to environmental protection for foreign investors. Nevertheless, the national industrial policy, as updated and revised periodically since 1992 with necessary reflection on the latest economic developments, industrial and foreign investment policy re-orientation and priorities, underscores the need for environmental protection and provides a guideline for pollution management applicable to both foreign and internal investors. The review of the previous policies, particularly the 2010 and 2022 National Industrial Policies, reflects some suggestions connected with environmental protection by investment projects or enterprises.

Firstly, it places a strong emphasis on the protection of the environment and directs manufacturing enterprises to control environmental pollution by setting up effluent treatment plants (ETPs) and common effluent treatment plants (CETPs) for strict compliance with environment-related laws and regulations.[10] It also suggests that the government adopt appropriate measures to assist private sector enterprises in managing their environmental operations and enable them to desist from activities that may cause environmental pollution.[11]

Secondly, the policy considers FDI not only as a means of complementing domestic resources for industrialisation but also as a source able to contribute to holistic development. It thus provides a condition for new technology to be brought in by foreign investors in the country, and strict screening of FDI will take place for that purpose. Foreign investors shall not be accorded permission to invest and conduct business in the country unless they bring in the latest technology.[12]

Thirdly, industrial policy has divided all industries broadly into two categories: thrust sector industries and regulated industries. There are almost 32 thrust sector industries in which investments are encouraged with lesser regulation and 22 regulated industries in which investments are restricted.[13] Investments in the regulated sectors are subject to a strict registration process under the Bangladesh Investment Development Authority (BIDA), Bangladesh Small and Cottage Industries Corporation (BSCIC) and Bangladesh Economic Zones Authority (BEZA). Registration by the said agencies is conditional on the prior express approval of the concerned ministry. The main regulatory issues of these industries concern the environment and worker health and safety.

The recently adopted National Industrial Policy 2022 has added more requirements for establishing environment-friendly industries applicable to national and foreign entrepreneurs. It has suggested establishing CETPs and dumping yards in every industry for waste management, dumping yard in every industry for waste management, green and climate mitigating industries, introduction of the 3R strategy and compliance with treaty obligations as well as local laws in case of ship-recycling.[14]

The policies adopted under the NIPs sound good and pragmatic as they reflect a lot of concentration on environmental issues in investment. However, the reality is that the condition for screening new technology, while in the policy directives, has yet to be translated into binding legal provisions. In addition, the division of industries seems to be based on economic perspectives and labour intensiveness. Government incentives are allocated largely to the thrust sectors as they contribute more national revenue, including the garments and leather industries. These industrial operations also have implications for the environment. However, the environmental regulation at the entry stage is concerned only with potentially risky sectors, not in general. Environmental regulation is a lesser concern in thrust sectors due to their economic benefit. The regulation criteria for the environment, health and safety need to be imposed irrespective of economic concerns.

The core legislation on the environment in Bangladesh is the *Environment Preservation Act 1995*, which establishes a legal framework for environmental regulation applicable to individuals and all local or foreign corporations. This Act is supported by the *Environment Conservation Rules 1997* for its proper implementation. The *Conservation Rules 1997* has been abrogated by the *Conservation Rules 2023*.[15] In addition to these two, plenty of environmental policies have been adopted so far in Bangladesh that act as soft directives for environmental protection, management and regulation. A good number of them have been adopted from a sectorial approach. The major policies include the National Environmental Policy 1992, the National Water Policy 1998, the

National Energy Policy 1996 and the Petroleum Policy 1995. All these efforts are intended to provide a sound regulatory regime for the environment.

To provide a sound regulation of investment-related environmental issues, the national legislation or policies on the environment should be a new generation environmental law or policy in recognition of the interlink between investment and development. It should be modelled on recognised international standards that ensure an environmentally sound investment. The new generation of environmental laws or policies underscores the need to integrate some essential regulatory elements in the legal or policy framework. The regulatory instrument mainly includes obligations relating to environmental impact assessment (EIA), a strategic management plan, social impact assessment (SIA), principles relating to an internationally standard waste management system and effective enforcement mechanisms (i.e., liability and compensation regime, environmental audit, effective administrative and judicial mechanisms). The simultaneous presence or interplay of these elements helps constitute a new generation of environmental legal regimes capable of sound environmental regulation and, thus, ultimately enables investment-induced development.

4.2.1 The Environmental Impact Assessment (EIA)

EIA generally covers the impact on the environment *per se* of a proposed project, as well as any specific risks associated with certain types of operations.[16] In the last couple of years, the understanding of this concept has been expanded to include social impacts such as the disruption of land use by indigenous people or forced resettlements that mostly appear in large infrastructural projects. EIA seems to be the best way to ensure that potential environmental impacts do not undermine the benefits of a proposed project. It can encourage the investors to consider the less environmentally harmful alternatives or identify a way to bring about a change in the project design to lessen environmental impact. It can also provide essential information for determining whether to place conditions on the project's operation in line with the forthcoming development objectives. Because of this, EIA is considered a procedural requirement laid down by international law[17] and incorporated into national laws, which is useful as an important tool for ensuring a holistic form of development through obtaining environmental sustainability.

Following the Stockholm Conference, Bangladesh's government, along with those of other developing countries, participated in the revolutionary process of protecting the environment by promulgating some ordinances, notably the *Water Pollution Control Ordinance* in 1973 and the *Environment Pollution Control Ordinance* in 1977. These two Ordinances did not focus on the application of EIA for controlling industrial pollution.

Later, an attempt to achieve overall environmental protection was undertaken with the adoption of the National Environmental Policy 1992. In the context of the vulnerable environment and climatic manifestations in the country, the policy was intended to achieve certain objectives of environmental protection and promotion leading to overall development. The main objectives,[18] therefore, are to:

1 identify and regulate activities that pollute and degrade the environment;
2 ensure environmentally sound development in all sectors;
3 ensure the sustainable, long-term and environmentally sound use of all national resources;
4 actively remain associated with all international environmental initiatives to the maximum possible extent.

In order to attain these objectives, the policy embraces all major related sectors that have operational implications for environmental pollution or damage, including agriculture, industry, health and sanitation, energy and fuel, water, land and forest. To control the potentially polluting character of investment, this policy, for the first time, introduces a mandatory EIA process, including a precautionary principle and a conservation and management policy. It necessitates undertaking EIA on new industries, new projects for exploration and the extraction of fuel and mineral resources and projects related to water resource development and flood control measures. Nevertheless, the policy does not create any statutory obligation for conducting EIA by the investors. However, this policy was an endeavour through which the government paid attention to the urgency of EIA in development projects. It was mainly out of the experience of environmental degradation resulting from industrial and agricultural development projects, particularly during the 1970s and 1980s, when the government took on many industrial and agricultural development projects without due concern and attention to their environmental consequences.[19]

The obligation for EIA first came with the enactment of the *Environment Conservation Act 1995* and *Environment Conservation Rules 2023*. The *Environment Conservation Act* provides for substantive obligations pertaining to the environmental management of industries. As part of this, it imposes an obligation on all industrial projects, whether private or public, local or foreign, to obtain an Environmental Clearance Certificate (ECC) for the project's approval from the DoE. Section 12 of the *Act* stipulates that no industrial unit or project shall be established or undertaken without environmental clearance from the DoE in the manner prescribed by the rules, and any person affected or likely to be affected by such activities can apply to the Director General of the DoE seeking remedy of environmental pollution or degradation. The submission of EIA by the project proponent is one of the procedural requirements for obtaining ECC. However, there is no direct or specific principle requiring the submission of an EIA report to obtain the certificate.

As a procedural requirement for ECC, the investors or entrepreneurs are responsible for commissioning EIA. The concerned environmental authorities review and examine each EIA document, its completeness and objectivity. However, the limitation of the Act is that it does not set any standards and parameters for reviewing EIA and management elements the environmental clearance should rely upon. However, clause 2 (f) of section 20 requires that rules be made to evaluate and review the EIA of various projects and activities, and procedures must be established for approval. In furtherance of these objectives, the *ECR 1997* was first promulgated and replaced later by the Rules 2023. According to ECR, the responsibility to review EIAs to issue an ECC is entrusted to DoE, the main administrative agency for environmental governance in Bangladesh.

With regard to the obligation of an EIA, the ECR 2023 categorises all industries into four: Green, Amber A, Amber B and Red, in consideration of the environmental impact (e.g., low, medium and high) of their activities and location.[20] The Green category is the lowest in rank, and the Red is the highest in rank regarding the negative impact of their activities on the environment. The industrial projects of Green and Amber A are exempted from initial environmental examination (IEE) and EIA.[21] A mere "no objection certificate" from the local authority is sufficient for a project to obtain environmental clearance and embark upon further activities. Only an IEE is essential for category Amber B to obtain an ECC.[22] An IEE and EIA are obligatory for a new industrial project falling under the Red category of industries for granting an ECC.[23] However, red-category projects also require a site clearance certificate before they can be applied for an ECC.

An EIA is carried out pursuant to the EIA *Guidelines for Industries* prepared by the DoE that include three major stages, namely, screening/scoping, identification of significant environmental issues and method of resolution and adequacy of the mitigating measures and environmental management plan (EMP). The recommended steps by the DoE are almost similar to those mentioned in all literature, such as a baseline study (similar to scoping), impact identification, impact prediction, impact evaluation, mitigation measures, monitoring programmes, risk assessments and resettlement and rehabilitation studies.[24] The normative screening process enables the DoE and the investors to decide on the appropriate steps to be followed in the environmental clearance process. Special emphasis is placed on site selection for industries with significant potential for environmental impacts, and investors must consider alternative sites considering the criteria put forward by the DoE.[25]

Risk assessment is an important part of EIA for a new project, particularly for mining and extractive activities. Recent incidents such as the Tengratila gas field blowout and the Magur Chara blowout in Bangladesh evidence the failure of risk assessment in projects due to corporate negligence, which calls for stronger regulation of conducting EIA to improve corporate accountability.

Access to information and the consent of the people proximate to the proposed project was not considered as a legal requirement of the EIA process in the *Conservation Rules of 1997*; it has been given a binding effect under the current Rules of 2023.[26] However, the local people's right to be informed about the nature of the project and its potential environmental and social impacts on them was respected before. The introduction of such an issue in the EIA process globally is intended to allow local people to take the opportunity to voice their views about the merits and demerits of new entrepreneurship from their point of view. The decision-making authority for granting approval or permission must respect the public comment and consider it before making a final decision. This process ensures community participation in the decision-making process for development. This is very much essential for a community-driven environmental regulation of investment. The DoE recommended public consultation in its EIA guideline, but not as a mandatory requirement and there is no pre-approval communication process with the public about proposed projects. But now, DoE requires this as part of the EIA process.

There is much past evidence that public consultation was duly held, but public opinion was not considered when issuing clearance certificates by the DoE. The incident of the Phulbari Coal Mining Project[27] in Bangladesh is one example of a project proposed through foreign investment that sparked an enormous and violent mass protest by the locals against setting up the project. It is reported that the proponent Asia Energy was issued an ECC even before the EIA report was submitted.[28] The report virtually avoided the public consent requirement. The investor claimed that a public consultation meeting was held, but the people's views were not published. The government of Bangladesh acted dictatorially, undermining the people's view and consenting to the project.[29] Following this, the people of the locality of the Phulbari Coal Mining Project expressed their frustration through a violent protest.

The avoidance of consultation with the people or ignoring their views is attributed to the absence of a binding legal requirement for public participation and the disclosure of information at the pre-approval stage. In addition, there is also no legal obligation to present investment proposals for public opinion and scrutiny. As a result, any mass opposition or civil reaction always occurred after the post-approval situation. The government always stood in favour of foreign entrepreneurs or development partners with administrative support, which the local people lacked. However, due to the change in the recent law where seeking public opinion has been declared mandatory, the situation would be changed.

4.2.2 Waste Management Policies

Waste management is an important matter for environmental regulation of foreign or local investment at the operational level. The need for industrial waste management is underscored in national laws and the international environmental legal regime.[30] Even the international multi-stakeholder codes of conduct provide principles and guidelines for waste regulation, and thus it becomes a crucial part of the sustainability reporting system famously known as the "Global Reporting Initiatives".[31]

For waste management, the concept of the 3Rs principles (Reduce, Reuse and Recycle) has been developed and pursued in the environmental legal regime. The 3Rs principles are used as guiding principles for waste management at the levels of the process of production and post-production. They encourage not only the prevention of potential pollution risks at the source level but also the sustainable use of all kinds of waste, such as hazardous, solid and water waste.

In addition to the 3Rs principles, two other methods have been developed that are also used for environmental waste management, namely, the environmental sound management system (ESM) and cleaner production. The ESM is a comprehensive system for sound environmental management that includes waste management in production and post-production situations. The different OECD conferences (i.e., Cancun, Wien and Washington) define ESM as a scheme for ensuring that wastes and used and scrap materials are managed in a manner that will save natural resources and protect human health and the environment against adverse effects that may result from such wastes and materials.[32] The ESM primarily encouraged the OECD member states. The ESM practice has spread over developing countries since the Basel Convention, which has explained this,[33] and most developing countries have ratified the Basel Convention. It is meant to control the cross-border movement of hazardous waste and internal industrial waste management.

The concept of Cleaner Production was introduced by the United Nations Environment Programme (UNEP) and is defined as "the continuous application of an integrated preventive environmental strategy applied to processes, production and services to increase eco-efficiency and reduce risks to humans and the environment".[34] The associated activities of this system involve measures relating to pollution prevention, source reduction, waste minimisation and reuse of waste products. One of the major focuses of this process is waste management through recycling as the eventual goal of cleaner production is to achieve a "closed loop" operation in which all excess materials are recycled back into the process.

The concern for a 3R process is reflected in general law on the protection of the environment and in specific waste management laws and regulations both in developed and developing countries. Specific waste management laws exist in the UK, the US, Germany, Switzerland and Australia.[35] Among the developing countries, Singapore, China and Malaysia have developed a legal framework for industrial waste management. Some countries, such as China, have adopted laws to promote cleaner production processes. The legal framework at the national level usually addresses the production process, responsibility for waste management, mechanisms for waste management and governmental responsibility for enforcement.

Therefore, the legal framework, in particular, applies to waste producers, such as industrial companies, waste carriers and waste disposal companies that operate in dumping sites. The main philosophy behind such development is to achieve ecologically sustainable development with waste management.

Bangladesh has no specific waste management law, and the 3Rs principles are not pursued comprehensively in the existing environmental legal framework established by the ECA 1995 and the ECR 2023. The mandatory requirement of submitting the layout of establishing an ETP for Red category industries is an application of the 3Rs principles under the ECR 1997. However, the Draft National Solid Waste Management Handling Rule, 2011, has used the 3Rs principle for solid waste management only. In addition, the National 3R strategy adopted in 2010 has made source segregation mandatory and given directives to local governments to pursue organic waste recycling projects.

Although the obligation for an ETP is established for obtaining an ECC and validity for continued operation, the articulation of the obligation lacks clarity on its legal status as there is no specific principle directing the establishment of an ETP. The wording of section 7 of the ECR reveals that the EMP should contain a layout plan, including the location for the effluent disposal system and the plan and design of the ETP with full information about its effectiveness.[36] Moreover, there is no clear mention that failure to establish an ETP results in rejecting an ECC. Without an ECC, industrial projects are not permitted to start trial production, and other non-industrial projects are not allowed to begin operations.

The lack of a specific principle for establishing an ETP creates uncertainty about the responsible performance of local or foreign operating companies. As a result, factories confine their commitments to paperwork only. A study on the tanning industry in Bangladesh, an environmentally sensitive sector, reveals that except for Bata Shoe Company (Bangladesh) and the Dhaka Leather Complex, none of the tanneries has a treatment plant.[37] Most waste and effluents are left for natural decomposition in the environment, causing serious pollution problems that affect the soil, water, air and human life.[38]

In addition to the lack of specific provisions, the legal deficit for administrative control through monitoring and inspection and accountability for violations creates a big challenge for its effective functioning.[39] Entrepreneurs are often reluctant to invest money in properly treating effluents, considering it a non-productive use of money. Sometimes, where industries already have ETPs, there is an unwillingness to operate the plant properly because of high running costs. It is, therefore, reported that there is a flagrant violation of law in this sector.[40] Industries discharge untreated chemical and chemical waste containing heavy metals into inland water bodies and agricultural lands almost regularly.[41] This situation cannot be improved without strengthening the legal regime for treating effluents and strict monitoring.

The important point concerning waste management and its proper regulation is that the existing legal framework is very insufficient and inarticulate. There is no particular chapter for waste management focusing on the different types of waste, such as hazardous, solid and wastewater, along with the responsibilities of the producers, owners and enforcing authority. However, the *ECR 2023* recommends waste disposal standards for mainly industrial waste in the annexed schedule 10, where emphasis has been placed on compliance with the standards from when the industry starts trial production or, in other cases, from when a project begins operation. However, the obligation for noncompliance for the entrepreneurs is not determined. Hence, the overall judgement is that the existing waste management regime in the legal framework in Bangladesh is inadequate compared with contemporary developments in this area.

4.2.3 Environmental Audit and Compliance Monitoring

Environmental audits are a vital element for enforcing environmental regulations, which are carried out during the operational stage of corporations. It has become a standard activity for corporate and non-corporate entities worldwide, mainly intended to evaluate the environmental performance of operations and identify and quantify any environmental liabilities at a site, such as past environmental damage.[42] It is also used to check compliance with established and proposed regulations, evaluate property transfer, establish existing levels of air pollution, water pollution and hazardous waste and satisfy the environmental requirements of lending institutions worldwide. Thus, the environmental audit system has become integral to many comprehensive environmental programmes. Its goal is to propose measures to address the environmental problems identified during an audit.

As in the EIA process, environmental audits for FDI performance have been undertaken as a mandatory issue in many countries. Mexico has adopted a national programme of environmental audits for over 15 years to control industrial pollution.[43] Mexico, at the beginning of the 1990s, developed a legal framework focusing on industrial pollution, but it lacked addressing environmental problems caused by inadequate management of natural resources and non-industrial pollution.[44] To resolve this problem, the Mexican government adopted an institutional framework concerning environmental audits. In some East European countries, the environmental audit is a common practice in private and foreign investments, contingent on social, environmental and investment commitments.[45]

The environmental audit is introduced in the national environment regulatory framework as a step to measure compliance with the EIA report and EMP. It, therefore, takes place following the EIA and EMP being submitted to the environmental regulatory authority. The methodology, therefore, includes the review of the EIA and EMP, observations on the environmental performance of the industrial plant and health safety aspects and meetings with management and technical staff. The setting of audit standards varies from state to state. Authorities and businesses can also apply the voluntary environmental audit techniques designed by ISO 14001 to assess potential FDI ventures.[46]

In Bangladesh, there is no explicit principle of environmental audit as a means of environmental regulation either in ECA 1995 or the recently repealed ECR of 1997 and ECR 2023. The requirement for environmental audit can be inferred from the provision relating to the validity of an ECC. Certificates for all categories of industries must be renewed, with some expiring after one year and some after three years. The renewal process depends upon an annual audit. The DoE has introduced a monitoring and reporting system that its official inspectors carry out to examine the sources of possible effluents and mitigation of environmental pollution, and based on their inspection report, the renewal order is issued. As there is no general criterion prescribed by the ECR 2023, the renewal process often is merely a carrying out of paperwork without maintaining proper evaluation standards.

Apart from annual audits for renewal, there is no legal requirement for regular or emergency environmental audits or monitoring of corporate activities. Regular auditing can suggest ways to minimise potential risks and improve techniques for remedying them. A study observes that regular audits could have identified the extent of the problem and established the most appropriate techniques for remedying the situation in three disastrous incidents in Bangladesh, namely, *Magur Chara*, *Tengratila* and *Phulbari* coal mines.[47] For example, it was known for some time that there were gas leaks at the *Phulbari* coal mine and that they were posing a serious threat to the environment and health of local communities.

Nevertheless, due to the absence of a legal requirement for formal auditing, there is no specific plan at the government level for conducting a general environmental audit for investment projects. Voluntary level auditing is still in its infancy and very much limited to a small number of large multinationals and the sectors that have a global market. Their in-home and external auditing activities are mainly meant to retain their corporate image in the global market without any obligation to local stakeholders. So, considering the need for environmental auditing for sustainable environmental protection, it should be integrated as a legal requirement and conducted periodically to review the effectiveness of environmental management under the existing legal regime in Bangladesh.

4.2.4 Accountability and Compensation Measures

A liability and compensation regime for environmental damage is necessarily an integral part of good national legislation for environmental conservation and management. The determination of liability can be seen as a means of legal compliance. It is a mechanism for implementing a "Polluter Pays Principle".[48] The rational point of introducing a liability regime into legislation is to ensure that the persons or corporate bodies responsible for non-compliance resulting in environmental damage face the prospect of paying for restoration of the affected environment or compensating for the damage caused.[49] The other purpose it mainly serves is that it acts as a means of penalising wrongful conduct and thus deterring environmental wrongful conduct and preventing environmental damage.[50]

For formulating a liability regime, the national system is normally linked to the existing environmental regulation and traditionally confined to penalty and compensation. The liability regime under the ECA 1995 in Bangladesh provides a mixed approach. The liability issue covers all procedural non-compliance that causes personal and environmental damage. In determining liability for causing damage to the environment, it has adopted some remedial measures. For example, it imposes restrictions on the manufacture and sale of articles injurious to the environment, prohibits an act or omission that may cause direct or indirect injury to the ecosystem and imposes responsibility for the discharging of excessive environmental pollutants.[51] The restriction on manufacture is exclusively for goods made of polythene, polyethylene or polypropylene. Non-compliance with these responsibilities incurs penal and compensable liability as detailed in section 15 of ECA 1995.[52] The penal and compensation standards rely on common law traditions applied in environmental offences. Non-compliance and the consequential damage it incurs do not amount to civil liability under this law, irrespective of the actors, either individuals or companies.[53] Therefore, the amount of compensation is fixed here as an alternative to prescribed sentencing, not considering the amount of damage to the environment itself.

However, in the case of injury to the ecosystem under section 7 of the ECA 1995, the director general of the DoE is empowered to determine the compensation for damage and direct the actor to pay for it or direct him to take corrective measures. The non-compliance with the direction of the director general will be subject to penal sanction under section 15(5). The director general is also empowered to file a suit against the actor in the competent court for the realisation of the compensation or file a criminal case for non-compliance with the direction. For compensation, the director general may engage any specialist or other persons.

The underlying principle of section 7 provides scope for the calculation of the compensation in consideration of the environmental damage itself. Another evidence for the consideration of environmental damage in the determination of compensation concerning water pollution is available in the *National Water Policy 1998* as it states that industrial polluters will be required under law to pay for the clean-up of bodies of water polluted by them. There is nevertheless a gap in the text of section 7 that the principle for remedial measures for the ecosystem does not cover all components of environmental damage as injury to the ecosystem is a single component of the environment. It is better to rephrase it as a "remedial measure for environmental damage" to make it more comprehensive.

4.3 Regulatory Mechanism for Protecting Environment

4.3.1 Administrative Management

4.3.1.1 Ministerial Body for Coordination and Execution

In Bangladesh, the institutional arrangement for environmental management can be classified into apex-level and working-level institutions. Apex-level institutions consist of Ministries and chief executives involved in policymaking, reviewing plans and overall supervision. On the other hand, the working-level institutions are affiliated with the different concerned Ministries' work as technical arms of the ministry. They are responsible for implementing ministerial planning, management, monitoring and enforcement.

As an apex-level institution, the Ministry of Environment and Forest (MoEF) shoulders the overall administrative responsibilities of environmental management and protection. In managing and shaping the entire environmental sector and in the implementation of plans and policies, it works with the Planning Commission, Department of Forests, Department of Environment, Ministry of Agriculture, Ministry of Fisheries and Livestock, Ministry of Water Resources, Ministry of Energy, Ministry of Health and Family Welfare, Ministry of Education and Ministry of Housing and Public Works. The responsibility regime of MoEF includes:

1 The coordination of the activities of other institutions and ministries to ensure that environmental concerns are given due recognition in their development programmes and play a role in policy advice and assisting the implementation of action plans;
2 Reviewing and monitoring the impact of development activities on the environment across all investment sectors;
3 Designing and promulgating policies and regulations for the establishment of industries and other development activities for the conservation of the environment; and
4 The determination of safety and remedial measures to prevent accidents that may cause pollution of the environment.

However, it is pertinent to note that each ministry has its own policy and programme frameworks, which provide a basis for addressing fundamental issues of environmental management and protection.

Two other high-level committees have been formed under the sponsorship of MoEF: the National Environment Council (NEC), headed by the Prime Minister, and the Executive Committee of National Environment Council (ECNEC), headed by the Minister for the Ministry of Environment and Forest. These committees guide the sectoral Ministries and Agencies on matters of national environmental management. There are also sub-divisions of these committees at the local government level.

Despite different institutional arrangements, MoEF's performance in creating environmental sustainability is not reportedly satisfactory. Its role in implementing action plans is frequently thwarted due to the fragile coordination between MoEF, DoE and line ministries.[54] The inter-sectoral coordination between water, fish and forest sectors is weak.[55] As the "clearing house" of all line ministries for all development projects, it lacks institutional capacities in terms of the human, technological and financial resources necessary for the proper implementation of policies.[56] Moreover, it lacks the technical expertise to effectively assess and monitor projects for environmental impact, and therefore, no progress or suggestion has yet been achieved. MoEF, nevertheless, has gained some success in adopting some policy instruments in association with the line ministries, such as the National Water Management Plan, National Energy Policy, Actionable Policy Brief on Agriculture and Climate Change Strategy and Action Plan. However, it has not developed any specific policy regulation for establishing investment projects for industrial and non-industrial sustainable development purposes.

4.3.1.2 The Department of Environment (DoE)

4.3.1.2.1 DoE's POWERS AND FUNCTIONS

Aside from the apex-level institutions, there exist four main regulatory institutions for environmental conservation, including the DoE, the Forest Department (FD), the Water Resource Planning Organization (WARPO) and the Department of Fisheries. The DoE is the key institution mandated by the ECA 1995 that belongs to the overall jurisdiction for environmental planning, management, monitoring and enforcement.[57] Given its legal authority, it is responsible for enforcing environmental laws and rules and implementing MoEF policies, recommendations and reviews.

The DoE has a legal mandate for national environmental protection and conservation. This includes a wide range of activities such as assessing and monitoring development projects for their environmental impact, raising public awareness about environmental issues, controlling and monitoring industrial pollution, conducting EIAs and developing guidelines for activities that affect air quality, soil and water conservation, afforestation, wildlife, critical habitats, fisheries and other natural resources. Under the administrative measures of the pollution control of industries, DoE undertakes to[58]:

1 Evaluate and review applications submitted by existing and proposed industrial units and grant ECCs provided all conditions are complied with by the concerned units;
2 Monitor and examine sources of all possible effluents, publish reports thereon, ensure the mitigation of any environmental pollution and determine from time to time the standard limit;
3 Advising the Government on manufacturing processes and materials that may cause pollution;
4 Declare Ecologically Critical Areas where the ecosystem has degraded and reached a critical state, control which operations or processes can be initiated in that area and ensure regular dissemination of information regarding environmental pollution.

4.3.1.2.2 DoE's ROLE IN REVIEWING EIAs AND ISSUING ECCs

To issue ECCs, the DoE conducts environmental screening or reviews EIAs depending on the type of industries as prescribed by the ECR 2023. An EIA covers the IEE and detailed impact assessment under its guidelines formulated for this purpose. Formulating a set of guidelines for EIA for industries is one of its major contributions to the environmental management regime. These guidelines have set forth specific procedures for different sector-based industries and non-industrial projects, such as the EIA guidelines for cement, textile, pharmaceutical, coal mining and water sector development, and roads and bridges, as indicated earlier. The guidelines pursue international standards such as the World Bank (WB) EIA system. The guidelines for water sector development are based on donor guidelines, e.g., the World Bank and Asian Development Bank (ADB).[59]

The EIA system began to work as a method of screening a proposed industry (although not as a legal requirement) after the 1992 industrial policy was adopted, as this document, for the first time, contained a special clause pertaining to pollution control of industry as indicated earlier. It began to take appropriate measures for preventing environmental pollution and maintaining ecological balance. Pursuant to this, BIDA, as a requirement of the approval process for a new national or foreign investment, has added a condition in the sanction order to the effect that entrepreneurs will comply with the rules and regulations of the DoE about industrial pollution. All industries, either national or foreign, thus undergo the EIA procedural regulation to achieve the ECC by the DoE to launch their operation.

However, there is a parallel between the World Bank and the ADB in approving any development projects they fund. The World Bank and the ADB have their own EIA procedure, which they maintain for the approval of the projects. World Bank staffers, since 1989, have been under obligation to screen all new investment projects funded by them. The environmental section of the World Bank examines EIAs for approval according to their regional strategies and guidelines for funded projects. This is often perceived as a case of an organisation imposing unnecessary obstacles in the smooth implementation of development projects beyond national regulation. Similarly, the ADB maintains a separate examination procedure for the approval of EIA for any project funded by them in Bangladesh, as it has developed a new environmental and operational strategy for Bangladesh to address the major environmental problems with the categorisation of projects like the World Bank.[60] These kinds of activities by the donor agencies may lead to the creation of a dual standard in EIA quality and hinder the independent management of the DoE as the principal authority of development projects at the national level.

In addition to EIA, the DoE also provides for EMP after the EIA procedure is complete to mitigate project-induced negative environmental impacts and enhance the positive environmental impacts of the project interventions. Therefore, the management plan is implemented during the project period and also in the operation and maintenance period. The DoE has formulated an environmental management framework that includes mitigation and enhancement measures, compensation arrangements, environmental protection and monitoring activities, peoples' participation, responsibility and reporting framework, and organisational and institutional arrangement.

The DoE has only a legal mandate under ECA 1995 and ECR 2023 to conduct EIA and EMP for the environmental regulation of industries at the project and strategic levels. There is no legal mandate to conduct EIA and EMP in other non-industrial infrastructural projects or plants. Therefore, the DoE's formal preparation for EIA is mostly confined to manufacturing industries. However, the National Water Policy 1998 provides for maintaining a formal EIA process by the DoE in all water resource development projects.[61] For infrastructural development projects and mining, the DoE conducts an EIA and EMP based on an *ad hoc* procedure, as mentioned earlier. Therefore, it is contended that the application of an *ad hoc* procedure creates the potential for avoiding adequate EIA reporting and due implementation. This occurs mostly in the case of more environmentally sensitive investment projects where the government pays little attention to its ultimate development interest and overrides concerns about environmental protection.[62]

4.3.1.2.3 DoE's MONITORING REPORT PUBLICATIONS

To ensure the effective implementation of EMP, it is inevitable that a strong monitoring system be designed and carried out. This is because the environmental monitoring system provides information that acts as a basis for making management decisions during strategic and implementation stages. It also provides a basis for evaluating the efficacy of environmental screening, the categorisation process, the impact assessment process and mitigation and enhancement measures and suggests further necessary actions.

The DoE has developed an inspection and monitoring system for the implementation of environmental management, and therefore it designed a comprehensive manual in collaboration with the Canadian International Development Agency (CIDA) in 2008. According to this manual, inspection and monitoring are conducted by the DoE's Department of Inspection to verify compliance, investigate the suspected violators and use enforcement tools to obtain compliance.[63] To ensure an effective monitoring system, the manual has suggested pre- and post-investment inspection and monitoring arrangements applying efficient and standard monitoring procedures. All aspects of an inspector's compliance monitoring shall be guided by the Draft Directive for Enforcement and Compliance of ECA, 2023. Thus, the standardisation of the monitoring procedure in recent times testifies to the DoE's willingness to strengthen its role in enforcing the relevant laws and rules for environmental management established by the ECA 1995 and ECR 2023, although it does not prescribe a periodic monitoring schedule. It is, however, argued that the Department does not have regular monitoring capacity and arrangements.[64] This is mainly attributed to the inadequacy of logistic support and the lack of the required manpower and expertise.

Notably, the follow-up disclosure of monitoring reports has gained wide recognition in national environmental legislation recently as an element of effective environmental regulation. The DoE is legally mandated to publish and disseminate information on environmental pollution based on its monitoring and inspection.[65] However, the reality is that the data and information of the DoE are often not disclosed to the general public.[66] Even the compliance reports submitted to the DoE by all industries every year under the legal requirement are not made public.[67] Under such a situation, there is a potential chance of getting manipulated information due to malpractice by the DoE officials.[68] Moreover, the absence of information or manipulated information deprives people of their right to access information and hinders the process of rectification.

However, sometimes, the data and information on monitoring are posted on the Internet in such a way that it reaches particular environmental groups, not the public at large. This technical mode of dissemination prevents most people from understanding the consequences and implications. Therefore, the data and information on general monitoring need to be published regularly and in a comprehensive manner. However, the problem is that the mode of publication is absent in the relevant law; there is not even a provision under the ECR 1997 requiring EIA reports to be subjected to disclosure and public scrutiny.

4.4 Environmental Litigation

The scope of litigation for environmental harm and necessary judicial arrangements improve the enforcement of environmental laws and regulations and ensure the people's right to access environmental justice. The scope for litigation by the affected parties or recourse to the judiciary or judicial intervention can help reduce the environmental harm resulting from industrial or development activities simultaneously with administrative measures. The successful interplay of litigation and administrative measures creates a sustainable environmental regime.

In Bangladesh, environmental litigation, both of a civil and criminal nature, is legally recognised for individual victims, and the practice of judicial intervention by the apex court has emerged in recent years based on public interest litigation (PIL). The ECA 1995 provides a list of environmental offences[69] to be tried by competent criminal courts. An offence is defined as violating any provision or non-compliance with any direction under this Act. According to this Act, the right of prosecution or suit for compensation is not directly conferred upon the individual victims in case of violating any substantive principle causing environmental damage. It is said that the court will not take cognisance of an offence or suit for compensation without the written report from the Director General of DoE or any authorised inspector.[70] The victim should come through the Director General or authorised inspector with a request to accept a complaint about an offence or claim for compensation.[71] Such a provision, in a true sense, curtails individuals' right to access justice.

Apart from the scope of judicial enforcement by the traditional criminal court, further development has occurred through enacting the *Environmental Courts Act 2000* as a supplementary to the ECA 1995. This Act proposes to establish a special environmental court in each administrative division in Bangladesh with concurrent jurisdiction (i.e., to try both civil and criminal cases) and the basis of instituting a case is a violation of the "environmental law" as established by the ECA 1995 and the ECR 1997 and other environmental laws to be specified by the government in official notification.[72] However, the government has not yet declared any other environmental law to be dealt with by the environmental court. In addition, despite being a special type of court, it has no separate rules of procedure for adjudicating environmental cases. Based on the nature of the cases, it follows the procedures in the *Code of Criminal* Procedure *1862* and *the Code of Civil* Procedure *1994*.[73] The environment court indeed plays the role of the judicial enforcement body of the ECA 1995, and therefore, this Act affirms the same prosecution restriction for individual litigants.

Introducing a special environment court is undoubtedly a good way to enforce environmental protection, but courts cannot achieve stated goals due to certain factors. Firstly, the court is not composed of special judges having expertise on environmental issues, but the judges act here in addition to their general duties at the court of the same rank. Secondly, the court has no *suo moto* power to take environmental pollution issue and investigate it. Thirdly, the court depends on the Department of Environment to bring legal action. Same as under the ECA 1995, *the Environmental Court Act* 2000 provides that only a person authorised by the Director General of the Department of

Environment can inquire into matters for trial by the Court. The Court has no independent power to take any complaint directly from the aggrieved individuals.

The restriction on direct prosecution by the individual victims of environmental damage practically discourages the spontaneous exercise of the right to access justice. This is because the intermediary bureaucratic intervention between the complainant and the judicial court may delay the scope of legal remedies and create venues for potential corruption, administrative malpractice and political indulgence, particularly when the opposition polluters are financially powerful like foreign multinationals, big local companies and public sector companies. This provision may be a stumbling block in the effective functioning of the Court that requires it to be amended in the interest of environmental justice.

There is also a legal deficit in that under this legislation the DoE administration enjoys impunity for their irresponsible act or omission. There are no provisions in the ECA 1995 that define the liability of DoE officials for their negligent treatment, involvement in corruption for issuing Environmental Compliance Certificates (ECCs) without proper scrutiny of the EIA process and failure to perform statutory duties such as monitoring and regular inspection. These actions may eventually contribute to environmental damage. Even the jurisdiction of the court does not specify trying offences relating to non-compliance with EIA and EMP.

Despite the said shortcomings at the level of subordinate judiciary, it is, however, true that in Bangladesh, a landmark development has been achieved in recent times in the case of environmental litigation by the role of the Appellate Division (AD) of the Supreme Court. In the decision of the AD in the FAP-20 Case,[74] the people's right to the environment has been interpreted as a right to life under Articles 31 and 32[75] of the *Constitution of Bangladesh* and the jurisprudence of *locus standi* under Article 102[76] has been expanded with the recognition of the case for environmental violation as a PIL. As a result of this decision, a phenomenal development has occurred concerning environmental litigation. The scope of litigation has been broadened based on PIL against all environmental performance by the government authorities or their sponsor for approval of any local or foreign investment project that can potentially cause environmental damage.[77] Thus, it acts as an effective way of ensuring environmental protection.

However, two things need to be considered in the application of PIL. One relates to the enforcement of the decision flowing from PIL. Another is creating a check and balance for the application of PIL. If the enforcement does not keep pace with the jurisprudence, the whole process will become futile and counterproductive. Therefore, an effort must be made to ensure the expedient enforcement of orders. The recourse to PIL indeed broadens the scope of people's participation in environmental litigation, which ultimately leads to their participation in a sustainable development process. PIL as a tool has engendered an element of accountability and created space for a human face in development.[78] It can afford a viable mechanism for compliance with sustainable development norms and help the development process become more holistic.[79] However, as with any tool, there is the possibility of its abuse and misuse.[80] There is a tendency to use it to unnecessarily interfere with and oppose development projects for political or other reasons, including religious, cultural and personal reasons. Therefore, there should be checks, balances and limitations through the adoption of rules for the application of PIL so that it is steered towards the attainment of environmental sustainability, not the mere opposition of development projects.

4.5 Concluding Remarks

The core FDI-related laws in Bangladesh do not include the principles regarding investors' environmental performance. They only emphasise investors' rights without highlighting their responsibilities. However, since 1992, there has been a focus on environmental regulation of FDI in National Industrial Policies. While there are some commendable aspects, such as the requirement of importing new technology and categorising industries for regulation, it would be more effective if these were given legal status binding on investors.

The Model Bilateral Treaty of Bangladesh refers to environmental accountability, but it lacks the clarity and adequacy needed to create a concrete accountability regime. Nevertheless, it establishes a scope for negotiation on environmental accountability in future bilateral treaties. Indeed, Bangladesh does not have separate laws or standards for the environmental regulation of FDI or laws governing the environmental performance and accountability of companies. The main legal instruments regulating environmental issues of both local and foreign companies in relation to entry and operation are ECA 1995 and ECR 1997. While these legislations have some features of sound regulation, they are not perfect. A review of the framework related to ETP, EMP, waste management, compliance and enforcement mechanisms reveals that it is inadequate for ensuring effective environmental protection and attaining the desired development goal.

The EIA system adopted by the DoE needs improvement. The public participation element is not well-emphasised, and the strategic impact assessment (SIA) method is not properly accommodated. Environmental audits and compliance monitoring are incorporated as substantive principles in the law.

The institutional regulatory mechanisms also face different legal and practical shortcomings in enforcing environmental laws and policies. The lack of coordination among different committees and excessive reliance on paperwork are the main problems with the ministerial body. The ministerial committees suffer from the institutional incapacity to substantially address environmental problems. As for the DoE, while it has developed different methods for environmental regulation, such as a modern EIA method and an inspection and monitoring manual, there is still room for improvement. It has not yet adopted a permanent EIA method for mining and other infrastructure development-oriented activities of companies that may have a potentially adverse impact on the environment. Additionally, there is a lack of institutional capacity, inter-agency link, procedural inefficiency, lack of in-house efficient and skilled professionals and an overall lack of implementing capacity.

Establishing environmental courts is a good effort, but they suffer from different types of legal and provisional deficits and limitations and are not free from bureaucratic interference. The Environmental Courts need to be strengthened by expanding their jurisdiction to any violation of environmental laws, administrative negligence and the right of direct prosecution or litigation by the victims.

Notes

1 In 1969, the world had about 7,000 transnational corporations. In 1992, there were more than 37,000 TNCs and about 200,000 foreign affiliates, and in 1996, this figure rose to more than 44,500, which controlled more than 270,000 subsidiaries. In 2000, there were more than 62,000 TNCs and 820,000 foreign subsidiaries, and in 2008, the number of transnational corporations in the world amounted to 82,000, which controlled 810,000 subsidiaries. UNCTAD, *World Investment Report, Transnational Corporations Employment and Workplace* (1994) 15–17 <unctad.org/en/Docs/wir94ove.en.pdf> 10 March 2013; UNCTAD, *World Investment Report, Transnational Corporations, Agricultural Production and Development* (2009) 17 <unctad.org/en/Docs/Wir2009_en.pdf> 27 April 2024.

2 One example is the 1984 Bhopal gas tragedy caused by the subsidiary of the US chemical giant Union Carbide that left more than 5000 people dead, injured more than 500,000 and created other human and environmental disasters. See VP Nanda, 'Export of Hazardous Waste and Hazardous Technology: A Challenge for International Environmental Law' (1988) *Denver Journal of International Law and Policy* 155, 165–70.

3 See the *OECD Guidelines for Multinational Enterprises* (2000, updated in 2011), Ch. V <http://www.oecd.org/investment/mne/1922428.pdf> 10 March 2013; see *Agenda 21* (1992) s. III, Ch. 30 <http://sustainabledevelopment.un.org/content/documents/Agenda21.pdf> 26 April 2024.

4 For example, the *Interim Provisions on Guiding Foreign Investment Direction of China 1995*, the *Nigerian Mining and Minerals Act 2000*, the *Nigeria Oil and Gas Industry Content Development Act 2010*, the *Investment Act of 2007 (Indonesia)* and the *Nigeria Extractive Industries Transparency Initiative Act of 2007*.

5 The Tengratila blowout had a disastrous effect on the ecosystem of the surrounding region by destroying the dense vegetation, villages, agricultural lands and other properties. The soil of the region was seriously affected by the explosion. The soil not only lost its fertility but also became inappropriate for constructing heavy structures. See Omni Bangladesh, 'Tengratila Gas Explosion: Its Impact on Environment and Livelihood' <http://omnibd.blogpost.com.au/2013/04/tenratila-gas-explosion-its-impact-on.html> 27 April 2024. The Magur Chara blowout took

place on 14 June 1997 and wreaked havoc on the infrastructure and equipment, the environment and the locality, causing damage to the tune of Tk 4,500 crore. See *Summary of Enquiry Report on Magur Chara Gas Field Blow-out* (Prepared by the National Committee to Protect Oil, Gas, Mineral Resources, 2000) <http://ncbd.org/?p=250> 27 April 2024.

6 See for discussion Xian Guoming, Zhang Cheng, Zhang Yangui, Ge Shunqi and James X Zhan, 'The Interface between Foreign Direct Investment and the Environment: The Case of China' (Occasional Paper No. 3 as part of UNCTAD/DICM Project Cross Boarder Environmental management in Transnational Corporations, Copenhagen Business School, 1999) <www.cbs.dk/departments/iki/cbem> 24 April 2024.

7 *Interim Provisions for Guiding Foreign Investment* 1995 (China) art. 7 (2).

8 *Interim Provisions for Guiding Foreign Investment* 1995 (China) art. 10.

9 See, *the Regulation for the Implementation of the Chinese-Foreign Equity Joint Venture* 1983 (China) art. 5.

10 *The National Industrial Policy 2010 (Bangladesh)* Ch. 13 (titled 'Protection of the Environment'). <industrial-policy_revised-2010-Eng.pdf> 27 April 2024.

11 *The National Industrial Policy 2010 (Bangladesh)* Ch. 13 (titled 'Protection of the Environment'). <industrial-policy_revised-2010-Eng.pdf> 27 April 2024.

12 *The National Industrial Policy 2010 (Bangladesh)* Ch. 13 (titled 'Protection of the Environment'). <industrial-policy_revised-2010-Eng.pdf> 27 April 2024. See the section titled 'Policy toward Foreign Direct Investment'.

13 See, *the National Industrial Policy 2022* (Bangladesh) Ch. 3 <https://file-dhaka.portal.gov.bd> 27 April 2024.

14 See, *the National Industrial Policy 2022* (Bangladesh) Ch. 16 <https://file-dhaka.portal.gov.bd> 27 April 2024.

15 See the Conservation Rules 2023, sect. 40.

16 See Pacifca F Achieng Ogola, 'Environmental Impact Assessment General Procedures' (Presented at a Short Course II on Surface Exploration for Geothermal Resources organised by UNU-GTP and Ken Gen, 2–17 November 2007) <www.os.is/gogn/unu-gtp-sc/UNU-GTP-SC-05-28.pd> 26 April 2024.

17 International law principles are derived from some key agreements such as the *Convention on Environmental Impact Assessment in a Trans-boundary Context* (Espoo, 1991) *Rio Declaration* (1992), the *UN Convention on Climate Change and Biological Diversity* (1992), *Doha Ministerial Declaration* (1992), *UNECF (Aarhus) 1992* and the *Convention on Access to Information, Public Participation in Decision-making and Access to Justice in Environmental Matters*, 1998.

18 See *the National Environmental Policy 1992* (Bangladesh) Ch. 2.

19 Salim Momtaz, 'Environmental Impact Assessment in Bangladesh: A Critical Review' (2002) 22 *Environmental Impact Assessment Review* 163, 165.

20 See *the Environment Conservation Rules* 2023 (Bangladesh) s. 7.

21 See *the Environment Conservation Rules* 2023 (Bangladesh) s. 7(6a) & 6(b). Based on their location and impact on the environment, 16 types of industrial units or projects fall under the green category. There are 26 types of industries falling under the Amber A category. See *the Environment Conservation Rules* 2023 (Bangladesh) schedule 1.

22 See *the Environment Conservation Rules* 2023 (Bangladesh) s. 7(6c). Sixty-nine types of industries fall under the category Amber B, including garments, sweaters, leather production and fabric washing. See *the Environment Conservation Rules* 2023 (Bangladesh) schedule 1.

23 Sixty-nine industrial units or projects fall under the red category, including mining, chemical manufacturing and road and bridge construction. See *the Environment Conservation Rules* 2023 (Bangladesh) schedule 1.

24 Momtaz, above n 19, 167.

25 Momtaz, above n 19, 167.

26 The *Environment Conservation Rules*, 2023, s. 16.

27 Phulbari is one of the sub-districts of Dinajpur in Bangladesh, with a population of 151,939. Different communities, such as Santhals, Oraons, Mundas, Rajbonshis and Bengalis, reside in this locality.

28 Monoranjon Pegu, *The Phulbari Movement: Resisting Neo-liberalism in Bangladesh (Asian Institute for Human Rights, Thailand)* <https://www.academia.edu/4557940/The_Phulbari_Movement_Resisting_Neo_liberalism__in_Bangladesh> 27 April 2024; Asia Energy, *Bangladesh: Phulbari Coal Project: A Summary Impact Assessment Report* (2006). <http://www.adb.org/Documents/Environment/ban/39933-ban-sei.pdf> 27 April 2024.

29 Asia Energy, *Bangladesh: Phulbari Coal Project: A Summary Impact Assessment Report* (2006). <http://www.adb.org/Documents/Environment/ban/39933-ban-sei.pdf> 27 April 2024. In the recent case of the Rampal Coal Power Plant, a joint venture project between the National Thermal Power Corporation of India and the Bangladesh Power Development Board, the government of Bangladesh discarded the EIA's report on the potential negative environmental impact on the biggest mangrove, *Sundarbans*. It approved the project and unveiled the construction process with its counterpart government representative amid growing public protest. Even the government ignored Bangladesh High Court's showcase, "Why the construction of the plant should not be declared illegal". See 'Rampal Gets Rolling', *The Daily Star* (Dhaka, Bangladesh) 6 October 2013; see also Chaitany Kumer, 'Bangladesh Power Plant Struggle Calls for International Solidarity', *HuffPost World* (online), 29 September 2013; <http://www.huffingtonpost.com/chaitanya-kumar/bangladesh-power-plant-st_b_3983560.html> 27 April 2024; see also 'How The Rampal Coal Power Plant Will Destroy the Sunderbans', *Progress Bangladesh* (online), 8 October 2013 <http://ncbd.org/?p=794> 27 April 2024.

30 See the below note 33.

31 For example, ISO 14001 (environmental management system) and the World Business for Sustainable Development and Fair Trade, US, have set standards for waste management as part of a total environment management system.

32 See OECD, *Core Performance Elements for Environmentally Sound Management of Waste* (February 2003) <www.oecd.org/env/waste/39559085.pdf> 27 April 2024.

33 According to the *Basel Convention*, ESM means taking all practicable steps to ensure hazardous wastes or other wastes are managed in a manner that will protect human health and the environment against the adverse effects which may result from such wastes. See the *Basel Convention on the Control of Trans-boundary Movement of Hazardous Wastes and Their Disposal* (1989) art. 2(8) <archive.basel.int/text/documents.html> 24 April 2024.

34 See Aquatech (Environment, Economics and Information), *A Benchmark of Current Cleaner Production* (1997) Cleaner Industries Section, Environment Australia <www.environment.gov.au/archive/settlements/industry/corporate/eecp/pubs/benchmark.pdf> 24 April 2024.

35 For example, the *Resource Conservation and Recovery Act* 1976 in the US, the *Environmental Protection Act* 1990 in the UK, the *Waste Management Regulation* 2012 in the UK, the *EU Waste Management Framework Directive* and the *National Radioactive Management Act* 2012.

36 See Rafique Ahmed and Nick Harvey, 'Evaluation of Environmental Impact Assessment and Practice in Bangladesh' (2004) 22 (1) *Impact Assessment and Project Appraisal* 64, 74.

37 S M Imamul Haque, 'Critical Environmental Issues Relating to Tanning Industries in Bangladesh' in Naidu et al. (eds) *Towards Better Management of Soils Contaminated with Tannery Waste* (Tamil Nadu Agriculture University, India, 1998) 23.
38 S M Imamul Haque, 'Critical Environmental Issues Relating to Tanning Industries in Bangladesh' in Naidu et al. (eds) *Towards Better Management of Soils Contaminated with Tannery Waste* (Tamil Nadu Agriculture University, India, 1998) 23.
39 See Ministry of Environment and Forest, *Bangladesh National Report on Sustainable Development* (May 2012) <http://sustainabledevelopment.un.org/content/documents/981bangladesh.pdf> 27 April 2024.
40 See Ministry of Environment and Forest, *Bangladesh National Report on Sustainable Development* (May 2012) <http://sustainabledevelopment.un.org/content/documents/981bangladesh.pdf> 27 April 2024; see also Margot B News, 'Bangladesh Environmental Crisis Campaign' (16 June 2010) <http://margotbnews.wordpress.com/2010/06/16/bangladesh-environmental-crisi-cam...> 27 April 2024.
41 See Ministry of Environment and Forest, *Bangladesh National Report on Sustainable Development* (May 2012) <http://sustainabledevelopment.un.org/content/documents/981bangladesh.pdf> 27 April 2024; see also Margot B News, 'Bangladesh Environmental Crisis Campaign' (16 June 2010) <http://margotbnews.wordpress.com/2010/06/16/bangladesh-environmental-crisi-cam...> 27 April 2024.
42 Gretta Goldeman, 'The Environmental Implications of Foreign Direct Investment: Policies and Institutional Issues' in *OECD Foreign Direct Investment and Environment* (OECD publishing, 1999) <www.googlebook.com> 27 April 2024.
43 Ramon Alvarez-Larrauri and Ira Fogel, 'Environmental Audits as a Policy of State: 10 years of Experience in Mexico' (2008) 16 *Journal of Cleaner Production* 66.
44 Ramon Alvarez-Larrauri and Ira Fogel, 'Environmental Audits as a Policy of State: 10 years of Experience in Mexico' (2008) 16 *Journal of Cleaner Production* 66.
45 Goldeman, above n 42, 82.
46 The Life-Cycle-Analysis, Environmental Impact Assessment and Environmental Audit require investment in inspection, monitoring, regulation and enforcement to ensure effective implementation. See Global Environmental Management Initiatives (GEMI), *ISO 14001 Environmental Management System: Self-Assessment Checklist* (1996) <http.www.gemi.org> 24 April 2024.
47 Shawkat Alam and Abdullah Al Faruque, 'Tragedy of Gas and Coal Exploitation in Bangladesh: Towards Ensuring Corporate Environmental Accountability' (2009) 12 (1) *Asia Pacific Journal of Environmental Law* 117, 147.
48 This principle was originally adopted by the Organization for Economic Cooperation and Development (OECD) in 1972 and contemplates the internalisation of pollution-control costs. The principle was reaffirmed at the United Nations Conference on Environment and Development (UNCED or Earth Summit, 1992) and further confirmed in principle 16 of the *Rio Declaration*. See OECD, *Recommendation of the Council on Guiding Principles Concerning International Economic Aspects of Environmental Policies* (26 May 1972) <https://legalinstruments.oecd.org> 27 April 2024; see also the *Rio Declaration on Environment and Development* (1992) <http://www.unesco.org/education/nfsunesco/pdf/rio_e.pdf> 27 April 2024.
49 Stephen McCaffrey and Maria Cristina Zucca, 'Liability and Compensation Regimes Related to Environmental Damage' in *UNEP Training Manual on International Environmental Law* (UNEP, 2006) <https://www.unep.org.resources/report/unep-training-manual-international-environmental-law> 27April 2024.
50 Stephen McCaffrey and Maria Cristina Zucca, 'Liability and Compensation Regimes Related to Environmental Damage' in *UNEP Training Manual on International Environmental Law* (UNEP, 2006) <https://www.unep.org.resources/report/unep-training-manual-international-environmental-law> 27April 2024.

51 Stephen McCaffrey and Maria Cristina Zucca, 'Liability and Compensation Regimes Related to Environmental Damage' in *UNEP Training Manual on International Environmental Law* (UNEP, 2006) s. 9 <https://www.unep.org.resources/report/unep-training-manual-international-environmental-law> 27April 2024.

52 Section 15 lists nine offences relating to the violation of different provisions as provided by sections 2, 3, 4, 6, 6A, 7, 9(1), (2), (3), 12 of the *Environmental Conservation Act 1995.*

53 See *the Environment Conservation Act 1995* (Bangladesh) s.16. This section focuses on offences committed by companies, which include the whole range of failure to perform or non-compliance with duties under this Act.

54 Salahuddin M Aminuzzaman, 'Environment Policy of Bangladesh: A Case Studies of Ambitions Policy with Implementation Snag' (Paper presented to the South Asia Climate Change Forum, Monash University, Australia, 5–9 July 2010) <http://www.monash.edu.au/research/sustainability-institute/asia-projects/paper_salahuddin_aminuzzaman.pdf> 30 April 2024.

55 Salahuddin M Aminuzzaman, 'Environment Policy of Bangladesh: A Case Studies of Ambitions Policy with Implementation Snag' (Paper presented to the South Asia Climate Change Forum, Monash University, Australia, 5–9 July 2010) <http://www.monash.edu.au/research/sustainability-institute/asia-projects/paper_salahuddin_aminuzzaman.pdf> 30 April 2024.

56 Salahuddin M Aminuzzaman, 'Environment Policy of Bangladesh: A Case Studies of Ambitions Policy with Implementation Snag' (Paper presented to the South Asia Climate Change Forum, Monash University, Australia, 5–9 July 2010) <http://www.monash.edu.au/research/sustainability-institute/asia-projects/paper_salahuddin_aminuzzaman.pdf> 30 April 2024.

57 In 1977, the Environment Pollution Control Board was established in Bangladesh. Under this board, the Department of Pollution Control was formed in 1985. In 1989, a new Ministry of Environment and Forest was created, and the Department of Environmental Pollution Control was renamed the DoE and brought under the Ministry's control.

58 *The Environment Conservation Act 1995* (Bangladesh) s 4 (2).

59 Momtaz, above n 19, 167.

60 ADB projects are classified into three categories, namely, category A for significant impacts, category B for some impacts and category C for no impacts.

61 The government ignored the EIA report because of its interest in developing the Phulbaria Coal Mine Project and the recently approved Rampal Thermal Coal Power Plant. See Pegu, above n 28; Talukder Rasel Mahmud, 'Rampal Power Plant Violates Environmental Law', *The Daily Star* (Dhaka, Bangladesh) 2 October 2013.

62 Salahuddin M Aminuzzaman, 'Environment Policy of Bangladesh: A Case Studies of Ambitions Policy with Implementation Snag' (Paper presented to the South Asia Climate Change Forum, Monash University, Australia, 5–9 July, 2010).

63 See the *Inspection and Enforcement Manual 2008* (Department of Environment, Ministry of Environment and Forest, Bangladesh) s. 2.1 *<www.doe-bd.org/Enforcement_Manual.pdf>* 30 April 2024.

64 Khandaker Mainuddin, 'Environmental Governance in Bangladesh' in *Additional Studies on National Environmental Governance and Cross-sectoral Issues* (2008) <http://pub.iges.or.jp/modules/envirolib/upload/817/attach/eng_part3.pdf> 30 April 2024.

65 The *Environmental Conservation Act 1995* (Bangladesh) s. 4(2) (f).

66 S Rezwana Hasan, 'Environmental Governance in Bangladesh: An Assessment of Access to Information, Participation and Justice in Environmental Decision Making' (Working Paper, The Access Initiative Bangladesh Coalition, 2009).

67 S Rezwana Hasan, 'Environmental Governance in Bangladesh: An Assessment of Access to Information, Participation and Justice in Environmental Decision Making' (Working Paper, The Access Initiative Bangladesh Coalition, 2009).

68 S Rezwana Hasan, 'Environmental Governance in Bangladesh: An Assessment of Access to Information, Participation and Justice in Environmental Decision Making' (Working Paper, The Access Initiative Bangladesh Coalition, 2009).

69 *The Environment Conservation Act 1995* (Bangladesh), s. 15.

70 *The Environment Conservation Act 1995* (Bangladesh), s. 17.

71 *The Environment Court Act 2000* (Bangladesh).

72 *The Environment Court Act 2000* (Bangladesh), s. 5.

73 *The Environment Court Act 2000* (Bangladesh), s. 8(1).

74 *Dr. Mohiuddin Farooque v Bangladesh and Others* (1997) 49 DLR (AD) 1 (called as FAP-20 case).

75 It has been held that the "right to life" under Articles 31 and 32 of the Constitution not only means protection of life and limbs necessary for the full enjoyment of life but also includes, among others, the protection of health and normal longevity of an ordinary human being.

76 *The Constitution of the People's Republic of Bangladesh* (as modified up to 2013), Article 102 (1). The High Court Division, on the application of any person aggrieved, may give such directions or orders to any person or authority, including any person performing any function in connection with the affairs of the Republic, as may be appropriate for the enforcement of any of the fundamental rights conferred by Part III of this *Constitution.*

77 For example, the case of *Bangladesh Environmental Lawyers Association v Secretary, Ministry of Environment and Forest* concerned the neglect, misuse and lack of coordination by the government authorities concerning Sonadia Island, a precious forest area and rich ecosystem. Authorities were alleged to be preparing the land for industrial purposes that were destructive to the environment, e.g. shrimp cultivation, thereby destroying the habitat for fauna and flora and weakening natural disaster prevention benefits. Petition dated 10 October 2003 <www.elaw.org> 30 April 2024; in *Bangladesh Environmental Lawyers Association v. Bangladesh and Others*, the Supreme Court ordered to close the shipbreaking yards that were operating without the necessary environmental clearance and take actions to prevent future environmental harm including establishing a committee to ensure the regulations are created and followed. Writ petition number 3916, 2006, judgement delivered on 6 July 2006 unreported <www.clcbd.org/.../bangladesh-environmental-lawyers-association-bela-vs> 30 April 2024.

78 Shyami Fernando Puvimansinghe, 'Towards A Jurisprudence of Sustainable Development in South Asia: Litigation in the Public Interest' (2009) 10 (1) *Sustainable Development Law and Policy* 41, 48.

79 Shyami Fernando Puvimansinghe, 'Towards A Jurisprudence of Sustainable Development in South Asia: Litigation in the Public Interest' (2009) 10 (1) *Sustainable Development Law and Policy* 41, 48.

80 Shyami Fernando Puvimansinghe, 'Towards A Jurisprudence of Sustainable Development in South Asia: Litigation in the Public Interest' (2009) 10 (1) *Sustainable Development Law and Policy* 41, 48.

5 FDI and Human Rights Protection

5.1 Introduction

Protecting human rights has become a major concern in the trade-related laws and bilateral investment treaties (BITs) of host governments. The increasing negative impact of foreign direct investment (FDI) on human rights and the environment in emerging nations is driving this focus. Certain FDI activities in manufacturing, mining and development in third-world countries have significant social and human rights implications.[1] For example, in 1984, negligence related to FDI led to over 5,000 deaths and 500,000 injuries at the transnational corporations (TNC) subsidiary Union Carbide in Bhopal, India. It also resulted in catastrophic birth deformities in over 100,000 children, exposure to hazardous gas, economic hardship, extensive environmental destruction and immense human suffering.[2] In addition, in Asia and Africa, companies like Freeport McMoran in Indonesia, Royal Dutch Shell in Ogoniland, Nigeria, and Texaco in Ecuador have been reported to have violated human rights and harmed the environment.

FDI-induced projects may also infringe on freedom of association, involve forced labour, arbitrary hiring and firing and offer poor salaries and working conditions. Construction and extraction activities might result in forced evictions, violating human rights, particularly the right to adequate housing.[3] They also expose the community to other rights violations concerning land rights, the ability to earn a living and support a household and family, cultural connections, access to water, health care and education.[4] Furthermore, the environmental impact of mining and other extractive enterprises can have disastrous effects on a community's fresh water supply or food supplies, harming people's right to life, food, water and other natural resources.[5] These human rights issues highlight the imperative for international and host country legal obligations and accountability regarding investment corporations and agencies. While the positive impact of FDI on a country's development is widely acknowledged, its detrimental human rights effects hinder this objective. Therefore, host country and international legislation are essential to protect and promote human rights and maximise the benefits of FDI.

DOI: 10.4324/9781003469117-5

Host countries should have the authority to regulate the operations of investment corporations to protect human rights. The host state can do this in three main ways: (a) by establishing a specific accountability regime under FDI legislation and/or BIT provisions and (b) by enacting or strengthening the relevant legal framework covering human rights issues or (c) by enhancing implementation, enforcement and remedial measures. To evaluate a host state's capacity to regulate FDI activities that may affect labour rights, resettlement after forced eviction, the right to a clean environment and the preservation of natural resources, it is necessary to examine FDI laws and BITs, relevant national laws and their implementation and enforcement mechanisms.

Bangladesh has significantly attracted FDI in manufacturing, mining, energy and other development projects to stimulate its economy. FDI laws and numerous BITs establish mutual obligations for FDI operations. These laws regulate labour, mining, private and Indigenous land acquisition and reacquisition, and natural resource preservation and conservation policies. The adequacy of these legal tools for FDI operations, including human rights considerations and the presence of suitable enforcement mechanisms, are important aspects to consider.

5.2 Protection of Human Rights in FDI Operations in Bangladesh

The Constitution of Bangladesh, like most other countries, attributes the responsibility for protecting and promoting human rights only to the state. Part III of the Constitution reflects on the state or governmental responsibility for protecting and promoting human rights, recognising it as a violating factor.[6] The trend for attribution of responsibility to non-state entities such as corporations for the protection of human rights has not yet developed in general through state constitutions. The reason for this is based on a very common argument that corporations are unlikely to act in a manner that deliberately seeks to violate fundamental human rights[7] and that business organisations are not concerned with espousing such policies.[8] However, states are far more prone to act in a manner that violates fundamental rights, whether due to the abuse of power by law enforcement agencies or the effect of a concerted state policy. The constitutional process appears to treat corporations as quasi-public institutions and thus gives them constitutional status that they neither deserve nor need to be useful in the social order.[9] Extending such responsibility makes them appear equal in status with the state and more important than they should be. Rather, it is better to regulate them under private law as private entities and make them responsible for violating human rights through the normal operation of the law.

The primary responsibility for protecting human rights is indeed attributed to the states as recognised by international human rights treaties and endorsed by the respective state constitutions. This does not mean that attributing responsibility to corporations for the same will place them at a status equal to host states and thus undermine their status. This is because corporations are treated as independent legal actors under international law. In many cases, they violate human rights with the indirect support of the host state itself. In addition, there is a likelihood of sharing responsibility with the host states for violating human rights, where the corporate investment is shaped by a "joint venture" with the state. The host state government directly or indirectly indulges corporate human rights abuses in major development projects.[10] So, the extension of responsibility to corporations for the promotion and protection of human rights under the constitutional framework in certain areas will have immense significance for creating obligation and accountability for violation.

In the Constitution of Bangladesh, the protection of some labour and employment rights and property rights are guaranteed along with state responsibility for enforcement. The labour and employment rights include the prohibition of forced labour and[11] discrimination on the grounds of religion and other factors,[12] equality of opportunity in public employment,[13] the freedom of assembly and association,[14] and property rights.[15] In all these respects, a constitutional provision can be developed to ensure proper responsibility sharing by corporate entities with the state for violating human rights. If a corporation violates those rights, it will be directly liable for those violations individually. If it is a state-sponsored violation, the liability can be determined jointly with the host state. Instead of sharing responsibility, constitutional provisions can be introduced, placing the state at the heart of protecting human rights and the corporations' responsibility for violating human rights as a subordinate concern.

One can argue that there is no need to assign specific responsibility to corporations for violating fundamental rights under constitutional provisions. This is because the state's responsibility for protecting human rights has already been established in international agreements. The state has the authority to act against anyone, whether individuals or corporate entities, who violates these rights rather than waiting for violations by state agencies.

5.3 Regulating Labour Principles Attached to FDI Operation in Bangladesh

There is no separate legislation for labour regulation in FDI operations. The main legal instrument of labour regulation in Bangladesh is the *Bangladesh Labour Act 2006* (hereinafter called the BLA). This is the only Act that regulates labour issues in general, as it consolidates all previous laws respecting labour and employment after being revised in 2006.[16] The BLA applies to local and international entrepreneurship, affecting labour issues. In terms of jurisdictional extent, the law applies to all industrial and commercial establishments located in Bangladesh irrespective of the nationality or residential background of the entrepreneurs, either local or foreign. The industrial establishment as defined under the BLA includes all transport services, mining, quarry, gas field or oil field, plantation, factory, newspaper establishment and other infrastructural development establishments such as construction, reconstruction, repair, alteration or demolition of any building, road, tunnel, drain, canal or bridge and ship-breaking.[17] Likewise, the term commercial establishment includes all stock exchanges, brokerage offices, insurance offices, commercial undertakings of industry and agencies, etc.[18] The jurisdictional purview appears to be encompassing the sectors where FDI is involved.

Regarding labour issues, the BLA covers most labour and employment rights as per Bangladesh's commitment to international labour and human rights conventions. Interestingly, the BLA applies to all investment sectors except for industries located in Export Processing Zones (EPZs) (where most entrepreneurship is based on FDI) to the right to freedom of association and other industrial relations. The issues relating to trade unions and collective bargaining in EPZs were first dealt with by the *EPZ Workers Association and Industrial Relations Act, 2004*, as amended in 2010. The said Act was repealed by the *Bangladesh EPZ Labour Act 2019*.

5.3.1 Bangladesh's Obligation under ILO and Human Rights Conventions

Bangladesh has ratified 33 International Labour Organization (ILO) Conventions on labour and employment, including seven of all eight fundamental conventions.[19] Among all of the ILO conventions, eight are considered fundamental to rights at work.[20] The *ILO Declaration on Fundamental Principles and Rights at Work, 1998*, unanimously adopted by all ILO members, includes all of these core labour standards. With the adoption of the Declaration, the principles and standards for right at work have become binding on all ILO members. As an ILO member, Bangladesh has shown its commitment to core labour standards. These standards include the freedom of association and the effective recognition of the right to collective bargaining, the elimination of all forms of forced or compulsory labour, the elimination of child labour, the elimination of discrimination concerning employment and occupation and the right to minimum wages and mandated benefits.

Apart from Bangladesh's support for labour standards of ILO Conventions and Declaration of 1998, it has also ratified some binding human rights conventions where labour related rights are in focus and thus taken upon the obligation to implement these rights through legislative efforts. These human rights conventions are the International Covenant on Social and Political Rights (ICCPR), 1966, and the International Covenant on Economic, Social and Cultural Rights (ICESCR), 1966. The ICCPR prohibits all forms of forced and compulsory labour[21] and recognises the right to form an association[22] as an individual citizen of the state. The ICESCR gives a detailed picture of obligation to labour rights that include, *inter alia*, the right to form, establish and join a trade union; the right to fair wages and equal remuneration; the right to safe and healthy working conditions; and the right to equal opportunity in employment.[23] According to these conventions, as a ratifying state, Bangladesh is obliged to integrate all these standards of rights into its existing legal framework immediately or progressively and undertake appropriate measures for their implementation. The section below describes how the core labour legislation in Bangladesh has incorporated the core of the international principles related to industrial labour.

5.3.1.1 Right to Freedom of Association and Collective Bargaining

The newly adopted BLA recognises the freedom of association and the right to collective bargaining.[24] The international standard for these rights purports that workers' participation in forming unions, strikes and negotiating collectively with employers must be free. The relevant *ILO Convention of 1948* states that workers and employers shall have the right to establish and join the organisation of their own choice without previous authorisation.[25] In addition, the organisation shall have the right to draw up its constitutions and rules, to elect a representative with full freedom to organise its administration and activities and to formulate its programme.[26] The public authorities shall refrain from any interference which would restrict this right or impede the lawful exercise thereof.[27] Reviewing the relevant principles in the legislation reveals that the BLA pursues international standards in these respects.[28]

Initially, strict legal requirements made it difficult to start a trade union and become a member, which limited the right to form unions. Most of the restrictions involve the steps for getting union registration, worker membership and the activities of worker leaders. No union can be formed without permission from the authorities. The authorities can unilaterally end, suspend or cancel a trade union organisation.[29] Another basic requirement for registration is 30 per cent membership of the total number of workers in a particular firm. This requirement seems to discourage unionisation.[30] About the 30-person membership requirement, the ILO Committee of Experts on Conventions and Recommendations raised the question of the Act's compliance with the ILO Convention 1948. In a 2009 report, the Committee noted with deep regret that the Act does not contain any improvement in relation to trade unionisation from the previous legislations and in certain respects, it contains even further restrictions which stand opposed to the Convention.[31] Therefore, the Committee recommended lowering the minimum union membership requirement of 30 per cent of the total number of workers employed in an establishment.[32]

However, national policymakers did not entertain this recommendation.[33] Following the collapse of the Rana Plaza building in Saver of the Dhaka District in Bangladesh, the question of trade unionism came to the forefront, and a Cabinet meeting of the ministers decided to bring about changes in the existing *Labour Act*. They agreed upon a reduction in the membership requirement for registration. Accordingly, an amendment was adopted on 15 July 2013 to the existing Act in relation to freedom of association. Unfortunately, it didn't address the reduction of the membership requirement. Hence, it again became the subject of huge criticism from civil society and workers' organisations at home and abroad. Critics said the amendment was a whitewash, and indeed, the government has allegedly tried to change the laws in favour of employers, particularly ready-made garment (RMG) factory owners, despite the *Rana* Plaza and *Tazreen*-like incidents.[34]

Changes have been made to how trade unions are formed in industries with the recent amendment to the *Bangladesh Labour Act (Amendment) 2023*. Now, companies with 3000 workers can set up a trade union with the endorsement of 15 per cent of the workers, down from the previous requirement of 30 per cent. Businesses with less than 3000 employees need the signatures of 20 per cent of workers to form a trade union. Groups of companies can also form a trade union with just 20 per cent of their workers' signatures. Although the recent reduction in restrictions has encouraged unionisation, the previous requirements often discouraged workers from joining. Despite an increase in the trend for unionisation compared to the early 2000s, the number of unionised workers in industrial sectors remains lower than expected. According to the Danish Trade Union Agency's study, there were 37 national trade union federations in 2023, with 9,432 registered trade unions and approximately 2.8 million trade union members. However, a report from the Bangladesh Government, released by the ILO, indicated that the number of trade union members is 3.11 million.[35] The trend for unionisation in the growing garment sectors of Bangladesh has been disappointing, with minimal change after the Rana Plaza incident. The reluctance of both local and foreign employers to enforce these standards may be contributing to the low regard for unions among workers.[36]

Another legal issue of labour law that indirectly contributes to the low unionisation trend is the provision for forming a participation committee in industrial establishments.[37] This committee is representative of both employees and employers. It can be formed or remain active during the existence or non-existence of a trade union in a certain firm. Employers are more interested in the formation of a representative committee rather than in a trade union, which is solely worker-led. The representative committee is tasked with functions similar to those of trade unions.[38] Taking advantage of this legal provision, both local and foreign employers tend to form a representative committee as an alternative to a trade union to maintain the employer-worker relationship and dialogue in their industrial units. In addition, because of the downsizing of the public sector in Bangladesh, most workers in the private sector, especially in garments and apparel, prefer a representative committee over a trade union.[39] According to legal provisions, the committee is composed of equal representation of employers and workers. Employers are always dominant in decision-making, and with employers' hand-picked worker representatives, workers have no power to bargain over the terms and conditions of their employment.[40]

This opportunity is also available in the industries located in EPZs, which are usually the dominant base of foreign entrepreneurship. In Bangladesh, until 2004, the government maintained a double standard policy in enforcing workers' rights to the freedom of association and collective bargaining. The exercise of the right to freedom of association as incorporated under the BLA was solely confined to the workers engaging in firms or projects located in non-EPZ areas and was deliberately suppressed in EPZs. The legal safeguard was that the *Bangladesh Export Processing Zones Act 1980*, as amended in 1984, empowered the government to exempt such zones from the operation of certain laws, including the *Employment of Labour (Standing Order) Act 1965* and the *Industrial Ordinance 1969* that dealt with the requirement of the formation of trade unions.[41] Accordingly, in 1986, the government suspended the effectiveness of those labour laws in EPZs.[42] The main reason for restricting trade unions was to attract foreign investment.[43] The major objective of establishing EPZs is to boost foreign investment by ensuring the required infrastructural support and facilities for creating a favourable investment climate; the governmental policymakers thought that permission of trade unionism would hinder this objective and ultimately affect FDI. They attempted to justify the EPZ exemption from applying labour laws as an economic necessity for attracting foreign investment.[44] Thus, EPZs continued advertising the absence of union activity to attract foreign investment.[45]

This discriminatory labour practice was criticised by the American Labour Federation, AFL-CIO, in 2003, and it petitioned the US trade representative to deny special trade benefits like the "generalised scheme of preference" (GSP) unless Bangladesh revised this discriminatory policy.[46] On the other hand, foreign investors in EPZs, especially from Japan, Korea and Taiwan, played a negative role. They threatened to close down industries and withdraw their investment if trade unions were permitted.[47] Nevertheless, upon pressure from the AFL-CIO, several meetings were held between international development organisations and embassy representatives from the said countries. Finally, the Parliament of Bangladesh passed the *EPZ Workers Association and Industrial Relations Act* in 2004, granting limited workers' association rights in EPZs from 1 November 2006.[48] The association is called the EPZ Workers Representative and Welfare Association. However, the permission to form an association was subject to certain restrictions, which are tantamount to the utter violation of international standards.

The major restrictions under this Act include *inter alia* (a) the prohibition of the formation of workers' associations in industrial units established after its commencement,[49] (b) the permission of only one association in a zone,[50]

(c) allowing the government a ban on strikes until 31 October 2008,[51] and (d) the cancellation of registration without any severe ground.[52] Moreover, this Act does not afford guarantees against administrative interference with the right of workers to elect their representatives in full freedom as the election procedure is determined by the Bangladesh Export Processing Zone Authority (BEPZA).[53] It was criticised as incomplete but considered a step in the right direction.[54] The permission to form a workers' association with such restrictions contradicts Bangladesh's commitment to observe international standards by ratifying the *ILO Convention of 1948*. It is assumed that the nomenclature of the committee and the laxity in the legal framework by imposing different restrictions on the right to the freedom of association, disregarding international standards and Bangladesh's constitution, were mainly to satisfy foreign investors.

According to the ILO Tripartite Declaration 1976, it is not permitted to curtail fundamental labour rights as an incentive to attract foreign investment. It states that where the governments of host countries offer special incentives to attract foreign investment, these incentives should not include any limitation on workers' freedom of association or right to organise or bargain collectively.[55]

The *EPZ Workers Association and Industrial Relations Act* became the subject of severe criticism by the ILO Committee of Experts on Freedom of Association. The committee stated in its 2009 report that the Act contained numerous and significant restrictions and delays regarding the right to organise an association in EPZs and failed to comply with the ILO Convention of 1948 and the ILO Right to Organize and Collective Bargaining Convention of 1949.[56] It identified the legal principles inconsistent with ILO standards. It requested that the government take necessary measures to amend the relevant Act to conform with ILO standards established by the relevant conventions. Later, another legal development took place through the enactment of the *EPZ Workers Welfare Association and Industrial Relations 2010*, which repealed the Act of 2004. The legislation did not bring about any changes. It outlines establishing a welfare organisation in EPZ industries that is very similar to the provisions in the previously repealed legislation.[57] This is despite the government's commitment to gradually introducing trade unions and ensuring different organisational rights at each stage when the former legislation is adopted. It even creates certain further risks or barriers to the rise of trade unionisation in the EPZs. It imposes the restriction that a member of this welfare organisation is not allowed to have any relation to or be a member of any other political party.[58] The said Act has been repealed by the *EPZ Labour Act 2019*. Unfortunately, it reconfirmed that the welfare association, as established by the previous Act, didn't provide permission for trade unionism in the export zones. This restriction is opposed to the objective purpose and content of the right to freedom of association under the ICESCR and the International Covenant on Civil and Political Rights (ICCPR). It does not protect workers forming an association from the interference of their authorities. According to this law, the executive chairman of BEPZA is entrusted with the power to verify the application for the formation of the association, conduct the vote to fulfil the requirement and approve or reject the drafting of a charter for the committee.[59] The association does not have collective bargaining rights except for negotiation with the employer on working conditions and remuneration or payment for productivity enhancements.[60] The later Act does not contain any real improvement on the former legislation.

Given the current legal framework of trade unionisation applicable for both non-EPZ and EPZ areas, it can fairly be viewed that the international standards of a trade union are not properly pursued in the BLA 2006 and are virtually absent in EPZ workers' association law. The gaps or absence of trade unionisation in the legal framework negatively impacts all employment rights, such as low wages and unequal treatment, arbitrary terminations, unfair charging for misconduct, etc.[61] Although it was created to attract foreign investment, this kind of legal initiative is unacceptable as it allows MNCs to avoid compliance with international labour standards.

5.3.1.2 The Elimination of Child Labour

Child labour has been declared illegal by the ILO Convention No. 182, and the ratifying states are expected to bring about its "effective elimination".[62] The term "effective elimination" indicates taking immediate and comprehensive action by adopting legal instruments prohibiting the employment of children in any occupation or establishment as defined by the *Convention*. The elimination of child labour is directed to all of the worst forms of child labour, which have been categorised under Article 3 of the Convention itself. These categories include all forms of slavery, forced or compulsory labour, compulsory recruitment in armed conflict; use and procuring for prostitution and the production of pornography and pornographic performance; use or procuring for illicit activities such as the production and trafficking of drugs; and above all employment in a work which is by nature harmful to a child's health, safety and morals. The last form of all these categories may relate to investment and industrial activities.

Bangladesh has ratified the *ILO Convention 182 on Worst Forms of Child Labour*, and in line with the direction of this Convention, the BLA 2006 prohibits the employment of child labour in general. Section 34 of the BLA states that no child shall be employed or permitted to work in any occupation or establishment. The wording of the prohibition is not qualified by any form of labour as prescribed by the Convention.

Bangladesh has not yet ratified the *ILO Minimum Age Convention 1973*. Therefore, in contradiction with the international age standard, the BLA sets the minimum age for admission to work at 14. It permits a child above 12 to be employed in light work that does not risk his physical and mental development or interfere with his education.[63] It prohibits children from performing hazardous work, but the term "hazardous work" is not defined in the law. The International Trade Union Confederation (ITUC) reports that the Bangladesh government is working on a list of hazardous occupations and tasks.[64] It also prohibits children's parents or legal guardians from entering into a service agreement on behalf of the child.[65] The principle of prohibition is a means of regulating child labour on the part of the state and assigns responsibility for all kinds of industrial and non-industrial entrepreneurs not to employ child labour as part of protecting human rights and dignity.

The child labour prohibition certainly has implications for human rights protection in investment activities. The employment of children in the workforce causes them to miss out on many rights essential for their growth and development, such as their right to education. It may expose them to abuse, exploitation and vulnerability in terms of wages, working hours, safety and security because of their lack of skill and maturity. Child labour creates an adverse impact on the human capital development of an economy by depriving children of education. If children are well-educated, the future labour force will be better skilled, and a skilled labour force is an important determinant of FDI. To drive maximum benefits from foreign technologies, the importance of an educated labour force in the host economy is well established in the literature.[66] In this sense, foreign investors should extend their assistance to host states in abolishing child labour and also contribute to child labourers' rehabilitation programmes, although the percentage of child labour in manufacturing sectors to FDI is relatively small. Foreign firms are not directly hiring child labour, but their supply chains or associates are reportedly involved.[67]

5.3.1.3 Right to Equal Treatment in Employment and Occupation

Any discrimination in employment and occupation has been declared illegal under the ILO Discrimination (Employment and Occupation) Convention 1958. "Discrimination", as referred to in the Convention, purports to be any distinction, exclusion or preference based on the colour, race, gender, religion and national or social origin which has the effect of nullifying or impairing equality of opportunity and one's treatment in employment or occupation.[68] The prohibition of discrimination involves equal treatment regarding access or hiring, termination, the assignment of tasks and the enjoyment of equal rights and opportunities at work, such as pay, benefits, promotions, etc. Distinction based on an inherent requirement[69] is excluded from the prohibition.[70] Another ILO convention called the Equal Remuneration Convention 1951 specifically requires equal remuneration irrespective of gender.[71] These two Conventions have created obligations upon the ratifying states to eliminate discrimination in employment and occupation through legal and policy initiatives.

Equality in treatment has been recognised as a fundamental labour right through the *ILO Declaration on Fundamental Principles and Rights at Work 1998*.[72] This Declaration affirms that all ILO members, even those who have not ratified the ILO Conventions in this respect, should respect, promote and realise this fundamental principle.[73] Bangladesh has ratified both Conventions and is, accordingly, obliged to promote equal opportunity and treatment in employment and remuneration.

The Constitution of Bangladesh responds to this international labour standard. It recognises the equal opportunity of all citizens in employment or public office and denounces any employment discrimination on the grounds of religion, race, caste, sex and nationality.[74] However, the title of the respective article of the constitution, "equality of opportunity in public employment", creates an ambiguity about whether the principle applies to employment in private enterprises. According to the title of the article, service in private enterprises remains outside the purview of the prohibition. There is no separate provision in the constitution guaranteeing the protection of discrimination in private sectors. It may be a constitutional lacuna or an error in the text.

The question of equal treatment in employment, either public or private, has been settled in most instances through the integration of standards into the respective laws of some countries. For instance, the Labour Code of the Socialist Republic of Vietnam has recognised the right of every person to work and to freely choose any work without being discriminated against on the basis of his gender, race, social class, beliefs or religion.[75] The *Mozambican Labour Law of 2007* is very articulate in this context. Article 237 of this legislation defines the norms of the right to work, stating that the right to work applies to all citizens, with no discrimination of any nature and equality of opportunity in the choice of occupation or type of work is a fundamental principle.

There is no such general provision in the BLA 2006 or any other laws relating to employment and occupation in Bangladesh. Only section 345 of this Act reflects equal treatment for male and female workers in terms of determining wages and fixing a minimum pay rate.[76] Protection against discrimination under this law is focused on gender but not on other grounds of discrimination (e.g., race, religion, ethnicity and nationality) as per the said conventions. It is, however, noteworthy that the relevant principles for appointment to employment do not indicate any discrimination in practice on the said grounds or any other rights relating to working conditions.[77] The absence of a general principle pertaining to eliminating all kinds of discrimination is nevertheless a legal gap. This legal gap contrasts with international standards and constitutional provisions and, in practice, opens the scope for the misuse of international standards. For example, hiring foreign nationals by foreign investors for the same occupation as local workers but with a higher remuneration under the cover of procuring a skilled workforce is an inherent requirement. Hence, it does not fall under the definition of discrimination. In addition, applying gender-based discrimination only to wages and remuneration may create scope for discriminating against women in other respects. They can be discriminated against when it comes to hiring or promotion because of their higher rate of illiteracy.

Given the existing legal framework, both gender equality and equality on other grounds in employment need to be taken into consideration in a broader and more specific way. The equality issue is essential for development purposes. Gender equality has a positive correlation with the economic growth of a country. Gender inequality in employment lowers the average level of human capital in industry and, thus, in the long run, negatively impacts investment and growth.[78] Klasen rightly points out that equality has its merit in development, whether or not it is directly linked to economic growth.[79] The World Bank considers gender equality a development objective in its own right, and its absence can harm the level of human capital and the well-being of future generations.[80] It is also observed that growth and social development, which rests on the exploitation of women, is a pattern that threatens human resource development in the broader sense.[81]

5.3.1.4 Prohibition of Forced or Compulsory Labour

Forced labour is widely accepted as a human rights violation and prohibited in all international human rights documents, including the ILO Conventions. According to the *Forced Labour Convention 1930*, forced labour is defined as "all works or services which are exacted from any person under the menace of any penalty and for which the said person has not offered himself voluntarily".[82] The Abolition of Forced Labour Convention, 1957 prohibits forced and compulsory labour from being used or mobilised for development.[83] The ILO has accused the Myanmar military of using forced labour in a systematic manner for agriculture and infrastructural development projects where the US Company Unocal had been allegedly complicit as a joint-venture investor for the construction of the *Yadana* pipeline in Myanmar.[84] However, this form of forced labour is not directly linked to FDI in the host states.

Bangladesh has ratified the relevant Conventions, and accordingly, forced labour is declared illegal by the *Constitution of Bangladesh*. Article 34 of the Constitution states that all forms of forced labour are prohibited and any contravention of this provision shall be an offence and shall be punishable as per the law. The BLA has no specific principle prohibiting forced labour. However, concerning children in forced labour, the Act prohibits debt bondage, but only in respect of children under 14 years of age.[85] *The Penal Code* in Bangladesh prohibits forced labour and defines it as a punishable offence.[86]

5.3.1.5 Right to Minimum Wages

The right to minimum wages and other benefits such as leisure, maternity leave and compensation for accident and injury are mandated as fundamental labour rights by ILO Conventions and international human rights documents.[87]

Every person at work has the right to claim a minimum wage appropriate for his living standard. In recognition, the ILO's Minimum Wage Fixing Convention, 1970 imposes a legal obligation upon ratifying member states to establish a system of fixing minimum wages irrespective of their groups. It also prescribes the factors to consider when setting minimum wages for workers. The factors include the needs of workers and their families, the cost of living, social security benefits, relative living standards of other social groups and, above all, the requirements for their economic development.[88] The Convention also suggests that every member state should create a minimum wage fixing machinery adapted to national conditions and requirements, comprising the representatives of employers and workers, to fix the wage and adjust it occasionally.[89]

Bangladesh has responded well to international norms and standards regarding minimum wages. The BLA 2006 comprehensively addressed the issue of the worker's right to a minimum wage and its enforcement and regulation.[90] The law provides for the constitution of the national machinery to recommend fixing a minimum wage, considering the factors proposed by the respective ILO Convention, imposing an obligation upon the employers to comply with the minimum wage rate and prohibiting strong payment at a rate lower than the minimum.[91] Accordingly, a Minimum Wage Board has been established to represent employers and workers. The Board is empowered by the Government to recommend and reconsider a minimum wage rate for all or any class of workers.[92] The law directs the Board to consider factors such as the cost and standards of living, the cost of production, productivity, the economic price of products, business capability, the economic and social conditions of the country and the locality concerned and other relevant factors in recommending the minimum wage rate.[93] The factors appear to comply with international standards introduced in the ILO Minimum Wage Fixing Convention.[94] However, the international standards strike a reasonable balance between the interests of workers and employers, suggesting the consideration of factors relating to the needs of workers and the economic factors relating to the levels of productivity and maintaining a high level of employment.[95] However, a close look at the factors mentioned in Bangladesh's labour legislation finds that more attention is paid to the business interests of the employers. This paves the way for them to avoid appropriate consideration for the living standards of the workers on different business and economic grounds. However, under this law, employers and workers are given an equal right to object to a proposed minimum rate if it is inequitable.[96] In addition, the law introduces a periodic review system by the Board that considers the changes in determining factors of a minimum wage.[97]

Despite these developments in the legal framework, the compliance status is unsatisfactory and does not seem consistent with the law. For example, the minimum wage in the RMG industry of this country was 1,662.50 from

2006 to 2010, which changed to 6,350 in 2014 and 12,500 in 2023.[98] The wage structure reveals that no consideration of workers' family needs or living standards was taken in setting the rate. The Board did not make any recommendations for change during this period because of the changes in the determining factors. The principle relating to periodic review by the Board prescribes that based on any change in determining factors, the Board shall recommend a modification or revision of the minimum wage.[99] However, in practice, it depends upon the demand from the industry workers' representatives. Only the RMG sector workers' representatives and the international organisations are vocal about raising their monthly minimum salary. No other sectors reportedly have strong workers' representation. Therefore, the periodic recommendation for changes in minimum wages is only present in the RMG sector.[100]

The legal framework of minimum wages under labour law does not apply to EPZ workers. EPZs are exempted from this law by the formerly *BEPZA Act 1980*. The BEPZA had its guidelines for determining a minimum wage rate, including other service benefits. The BEPZA Instruction No. 2 laid down directives concerning setting minimum wages. According to this Instruction, the power to set the minimum wage was vested with the employers,[101] and the workers' association cannot interfere with the minimum wage in any unit of any EPZ area settled by the employers[102] except in the matters of increasing the wage and other benefits. There is no recommendation under the said Instruction for compliance with ILO considerations for setting minimum wages. As a result, in 2010, when re-fixing the minimum wage in different sectors such as garments, leather products and plastic products, it was revealed that from 1989 to 2010, the wage rate remained unchanged, which was extremely inadequate in maintaining a decent standard of living. For example, in the garment sector, for the lowest grade worker, the monthly minimum wage was $25–30, which means less than US$1.00 per day, and this is considered poor as per the international criteria.[103] No periodic revision was held during this period. This has been criticised as a violation of the fundamental human rights of the workers in EPZs.[104] The re-fixing of the minimum wage in 2010 for all grades from apprentice to high-skilled does not show any consideration for the cost of satisfying the basic needs of workers and their families. The increased salary rate is inconsistent with current commodity price rises, house rents and economic inflation.[105]

The laxity in the legal framework of minimum wages for EPZ workers in Bangladesh over two decades is responsible for the situation whereby foreign investors have generally paid lower wages within these enclaves than those paid in industries located outside but still within the same country.[106] However, the latest enacted separate labour law for EPZ, called the *EPZ Labour Act 2019*, made some changes regarding the minimum wages, such as the power of the government to form the EPZ Minimum Wages Board and the fixing of minimum wages for workers. Unfortunately, no attempt was made to implement this provision. Industries in the EPZs have indeed contributed to the increase in employment opportunities. Still, there has been no overall improvement in the living standards of the workers, who are the main stakeholders.

Conversely, some recent studies claim that foreign investors rarely violate workers' right to fair remuneration. They show that foreign investors pay higher wages to equivalent workers than their domestic-owned counterparts.[107] One prime example is a study based on ILO data in five East Asian countries (Hong Kong, Korea, Singapore, Thailand and the Philippines), which found that FDI raised overall wages in all countries.[108] The reason behind this may be the stringent national law provisions of those host countries. Therefore, in Bangladesh, all industries, irrespective of their location within or outside the EPZ, should be brought under the same legal framework of minimum wages in full compliance with international standards to ensure the fundamental rights of the workers that eventually may lead to the economic and social development of the country on the whole.

5.4 Regulating Occupational Safety and Health in FDI Operations in Bangladesh

Workers' rights to health, safety and security in the workplace are termed in the legal texts as their right to occupational safety and health (OSH). It is recognised as a fundamental labour and employment right by the human rights documents and ILO Conventions. A plethora of ILO Conventions and Recommendations[109] set forth the international standards of this right by defining principles in this field as well as allocating duties and responsibilities to the competent authorities, employers and workers. The international standards of OSH concern general protection measures (for example, guarding of machinery, medical examination of young workers or limiting the weight of loads to be transported by a single worker); protection in specific branches of economic activity (such as mining and building industry, commerce and dock work); protection of specific professions (for example, nurses and seafarers) and categories of workers having particular occupational health needs (such as women and young workers); protection against specific risks (ionising radiation, benzene, asbestos); prevention of occupational cancer; control of air pollution, noise and vibration in working environments; and measures to ensure safety in the use of chemicals including the prevention of major industrial accidents. As part of governmental and employers' duties, the *ILO Occupational Safety and Health Convention 1981* provides for the adoption of a national occupational safety and health policy, as well as describing the actions to be taken by governments and within enterprises to promote OSH to improve the working environment. The ILO Tripartite Declaration of Principles

Concerning Multinational Enterprises and Social Policy 1977 suggests MNCs maintain the highest standards of safety and health in conformity with national requirements.[110]

Bangladesh has not yet ratified two key conventions on OSH, the ILO Convention on Occupational Safety and Health, 1981 and the Promotional Framework for Occupational Safety and Health, 2006. However, the BLA 2006 focuses on many OSH standards recognised by the ILO Convention.

The legal framework of OSH in the BLA 2006 is quite extensive. The framework consists of three chapters. Chapter 5 addresses health and hygiene issues intended to ensure and improve a pollution-free working environment in the industries. The relevant principles deal with issues such as cleanliness, ventilation and temperature, removing dust and fumes, the disposal of waste and effluents, avoiding overcrowding, providing good lighting and drinking water and the establishment of latrines and urinals.[111] Chapter 6 provides guidelines for safety measures relating to building and machinery, the preparation of required precautionary measures and arrangements in the case of fire (such as escape exits, connecting stairways on each floor and active firefighting apparatus), safety from dangerous fumes, protection of eyes, availability of lifts, stairs and alternative exits and approaches, precautions against the use of chemicals, explosive or inflammable dust or gas and so on.[112] Chapter 7 mainly deals with implementation and enforcement mechanisms for workplace occupational safety and security provisions that cover the respective responsibilities of employers, the government and workers.[113] Under the BLA, the main tools for enforcing OSH provisions are inspection and inquiry, reporting, banning or prohibiting operations upon reporting any accident, occupational disease or dangerous operation of machinery. The Act also empowers the concerned authority to make rules for enforcing health and safety in the workplace.[114] In addition, the *Mines Act 1923* also sets a legal framework of OSH for mine workers in Bangladesh.[115]

Although in view of the legal provisions incorporated in the BLA, the labour law seems to be encompassing the OSH standards, due to some reason, huge gaps are noticeable in the law and practice. One intrinsically important thing is that in the Act, the terminology of OSH has not been used, and therefore, OSH as a fundamental right of the workers is not translated properly through the legal provisions. Because of the absence of the term OSH, the fundamental protective spirit and requirements are missing from the Act. Neighbouring state labour laws, such as the Nepalese Labour Act, covers OSH issues by fully applying the terminology itself. Thailand has a separate law titled the *Safety, Health and Work Place Act* (revised in 2011).

In addition to the state of the legal framework, the enforcement mechanism is not satisfactorily designed in the law. The OSH inspection system under the Act is poor, reportedly understaffed and corrupt, which casts corners of legal requirements. There is no specialised governmental department that deals specifically with OSH. Penal sanctions for violating OSH requirements are negligible for mega-corporations, who ignore requirements with impunity, often under political patronage and cover-up. This is evident from some recent disasters, namely, the collapse of the Rana Plaza building[116] and the fire in the Tazreen Fashion building[117] (a renowned garment factory), which reflects on vulnerable OSH situations and non-compliance with OSH standards. In these two cases, the governmental initiatives to apply justice to those responsible and compensate the victims have not been satisfactory. However, it is commendable that an amendment was made on 15 July 2013 to improve OSH situations at Bangladesh workplaces in the face of a volley of criticism from the international community, which termed the working situation there as slavery.

Along with legal development, strengthening the implementation mechanisms is important. Therefore, Bangladesh should ratify the ILO conventions on OSH, most importantly the one relating to a promotional framework, to be under international obligation to implement the standards consistent with its suggestions. It should also establish and activate the proposed National Council for Industrial OSH with broader responsibility.

5.5 Mechanisms for Enforcing Labour Principles and OSH Rights

The BLA 2006 introduces administrative and judicial mechanisms to ensure compliance with the law and enforce labour rights. The administrative system includes the Department of Labour, Department of Inspection and Department of Industrial Relations for EPZ. The judicial system includes the Labour Court, Labour Appellate Tribunal and the High Court Division (HCD) of the Supreme Court.

5.5.1 *The Administrative Mechanisms*

5.5.1.1 The Department of Labour

The BLA 2006 provides for the establishment of the Department of Labour headed by the Director of Labour with a required number of other directors appointed by the government to enforce compliance with the provisions of this Act.[118] According to the Act, their powers, among others, concern enforcing workers' right to a trade union. The prescribed functions include registering a trade union, lodging complaints with Labour Courts for action against any offence or unfair labour practice or violation of any provisions of laws relating to trade unionisation and acting as conciliator in any industrial dispute arising out of workers and their employment.[119] The duty for registration also extends to cancellation and rejection of the trade union registration, disqualification of membership, etc.

The power to lodge any offence concerning unfair labour practice is an effective tool that protects workers' right to a trade union and its exercise. Unfair labour practice, as defined by the Act, may be held by employers or workers and contains a long list of activities militating against the free exercise of the right to freedom of association. The constituent elements of unfair labour practice on the part of the employers involve activities leading to the violation of workers' right to a trade union.[120] On the other hand, unfair labour practices by the workers include intimidation, inducement and compelling or attempting to compel any worker to be or not to be in a trade union. By exercising administrative power in managing complaints related to trade union issues, the Director can contribute to facilitating the protection of workers' rights.

5.5.1.2 The Department of Inspection

The Department of Inspection, headed by a chief inspector and with the requisite number of deputy chief and assistant chief inspectors, is established under this Act to inspect compliance with its rights and obligations.[121] Inspection as a compliance mechanism includes the following types of responsibility regimes[122]:

1 The inspection or examination of the place and premises of the establishment at any reasonable time
2 The examination of papers of the business establishment or industry as to how far it is prepared or has progressed in accordance with the provisions of this Act
3 Making the necessary examinations and inquiries to ascertain compliance with the provisions of the Act, its rules and regulations regarding industry building or the establishment and the workers

The first category includes the inspection of matters relating to OSH arrangements available on the premises and in industry buildings. The second category concerns the company's compliance policy, code of conduct, reports, etc. The third category includes matters relating to employment rights, the payment of wages, hours of work and rest and prosecution against violating labour laws. It also includes the approval of building plans and construction and liaison with different governmental departments, employers and trade unions on enforcing labour laws.

As per the existing law, the Department of Inspection under the Ministry of Labour has been established to ensure the smooth and effective functioning of the inspection. To facilitate its functioning, it works under three wings: an engineering section, a general section and a medical section. The engineering section is responsible for occupational safety, accident investigation, compensation, etc. The general section deals with general welfare measures, the payment of wages, working hours and conditions of employment. The medical section is responsible for occupational health, hygiene and maternity benefits. Upon the inspection, the inspector from each section advises the management concerned on the spot on the rectifying of defects or infringements observed. He or she subsequently issues a notice, and during the follow-up inspection, if the required actions for defects and/or infringements are not taken, he or she files a lawsuit for violation in the labour court.

Although the inspection department is empowered with the approval of building construction upon inspection and the inspection of other health and safety measures in the firm or project, as per the schedule or on an emergency basis, the Act lacks rules regarding the inspection of these works vis-à-vis safety and other aspects of importance to workers. It also lacks principles relating to holding the inspectors accountable for their work. In addition, as this inspection system in the current labour law replaces the previous Factory Act 1965 inspection system, which has been merged with this law, the system is only designed for factories, not any other development project. However, the *Mine Act 1923* provides for the obligation of a chief inspector office to supervise working conditions in the mine and to ensure safety conditions. So, to remove the legal gaps, firstly, in the interest of the safety of factory workers, the law requires that the building owner submit a certificate to the concerned authorities following the approval of building work. Secondly, the jurisdiction of the inspector's office under the current labour law should be extended to development projects.

Notably, the current Labour Act suggests that the government establish the National Council for Industrial Health and Safety to ensure compliance with industrial health and safety issues.[123] The proposed council will be based on a multi-stakeholder framework, with the participation of employers and employees of different manufacturing sectors.[124] Its responsibility includes (1) preparing a national policy for ensuring safety in industrial establishments and maintaining the health and conditions of work and atmosphere and (2) framing guidelines for implementing its policy. The proposal for constituting such an institutional framework at the auspices of the government is a good endeavour to promote the conditions of occupational health and safety in Bangladesh, as we witness in the activities of the National Council for Occupational Health and Safety in Malaysia established under the *Occupational Health and Safety Act, 1994*. The government of Bangladesh has not yet constituted the Council.

5.5.1.3 Department of Industrial Relations for EPZ

The Department of Industrial Relations in EPZs is a substitute organisation for the Department of Labour and Chief Inspector of Factories under the BLA 2006. There are also 60 councillors appointed to provide technical assistance to this department to implement BEZA instructions 1 and 2, the newly repealed *EPZ Workers Society and Industrial Relations Act 2004*, the *EPZ*

Workers Welfare Society and Industrial Relation Act 2010 and *the Bangladesh EPZ Labour Act 2019*. This department is assigned many duties per the direction and guidelines of BEZA (formerly BEPZA), where there is no specific mention of workers' fundamental rights and working conditions. However, it is responsible for dispute settlement based on workers' complaints as per BEPZA rules and regulations. BEZA instructions 1 and 2 deal with paying wages and other welfare facilities and do not focus on working conditions. So the inspection and dispute settlement issues in the EPZs by the said department are not concerned with anything related to the recognised fundamental labour rights and right to OSH.

5.5.2 The Judicial Mechanism

5.5.2.1 The Labour Court

The Labour Court (LC) is a judicial mechanism established under this Act to enforce rights guaranteed or secured to any collective bargaining agent (CBA), employer or worker. The court shall have a chairman from the District Judge level and two other members to assist the chairman. One of the members will represent the workers and another of the employers.

The jurisdiction of the Court encompasses four main tasks, namely: (a) to adjudicate and determine an industrial dispute or any other dispute arising out of the violation of any provision of this Act and brought before the Court; (b) enquire into and adjudicate any matter relating to the implementation or violation of settlement which is referred to it by the Government; (c) try offences under this Act; and (d) exercise and perform such other powers and functions as are or may be conferred upon or assigned to it by or under this Act or any other law.[125]

The core objective of the LC is to settle industrial disputes. An industrial dispute involves disputes relating to labour rights and disputes relating to service interests. No differentiation is made between a right's dispute and an interest dispute under this law; both can be taken to the LC as a dispute. Any CBA, employer or worker can file a dispute with the LC on the grounds of violating any right conferred by the Act or any award by peaceful settlement through conciliation or arbitration.[126] Individual workers can bring a complaint to the court in the case of dismissal, retrenchment or removal from employment.[127] There is no alternative mechanism for settling individual disputes other than by the intervention of the LC. Individual disputes cannot be taken to court by the CBA as an industrial dispute. Considering this as a legal deficit in the jurisdiction of the court, this issue has been brought to the attention of the Supreme Court of Bangladesh. Still, the Court has clarified that the LC cannot entertain individual disputes as industrial disputes.[128]

It is commendable that the *Act* provides scope for an individual's direct access to justice under this court to uphold employment rights when they are violated. However, the limitation that an individual's dispute cannot be treated as an industrial dispute and, therefore, is not capable of being raised by the CBA to the court may create potential risks to ensuring an individual's right to seek remedies in a country such as Bangladesh where most workers are poor and unwilling to resort to litigation against their employers. So, disputes relating to the violation of individual rights can be introduced as industrial disputes on a case basis in the legal framework of dispute resolution under the law.

5.5.2.2 The Labour Appellate Tribunal

The BLA 2006 establishes the Labour Appellate Tribunal to hear the appeals from the LC. It consists of a chairman, or if the government deems fit, a chairman and such number of members as the government deems fit. The Labour Appellate Tribunal may set aside, vary or modify any award or decision in judgement or sentence given by the LC or send the case back to it. The creation of the Appellate Tribunal is a major contribution of the current Act as the predecessor labour laws lacked this provision and the judgement of the LC was final. Now, by introducing such a provision, the right to appeal of the aggrieved party has been ensured.

5.5.2.3 High Court Division of the Supreme Court

Even though the labour court has been entrusted with the exclusive jurisdiction in respect of deciding labour issues, the aggrieved person can invoke the jurisdiction of the HCD on the ground that the matter in issue leads to the violation of fundamental rights and there is no other efficacious remedy in this matter.[129] Before the constitution of the Appellate Tribunal under the BLA 2006, it was the only way to invoke the writ jurisdiction of the High Court Division of the Supreme Court of Bangladesh for challenging a decision passed by the LC. Now, despite the recourse to the Labour Appellate Tribunal, the jurisdiction of the High Court Division of the Supreme Court of Bangladesh can be invoked on the grounds of the violation of fundamental rights or any procedural error committed by the LC.

5.5.2.4 The EPZ Labour Tribunal and Appellate Tribunal

The adjudication system under the Labour Court and the Labour Appellate Tribunals does not apply first to EPZ cases. For the first time, the EPZ Workers' Association and Industrial Relations Act 2004 established the EPZ Labour Tribunal and EPZ Labour Appellate Tribunal to settle the disputes or try the offences under this Act. Before the enactment of this law, the conciliation or arbitration method was used to settle labour disputes. This was controversial for being primarily investor-biased.[130] This Act provides the governmental obligation to establish an EPZ Labour Tribunal in every EPZ.[131] However, no tribunal has been established since the enactment until it was repealed by the EPZ Workers Welfare Association and Industrial Relations 2010. The new *Act of 2010* stipulates similar provisions for establishing the Labour Tribunal and Appellate Tribunal in each EPZ.[132] The establishment of the Labour Tribunal is still being processed, and until now, no EPZ tribunal has been established.[133] The latest enactment of 2019, which repealed the previous Act of 2010, also provided similar provisions, but no separate judicial mechanism has been established. But it provided the option of invoking the jurisdiction of the Labour Court and Appellate Tribunal until any separate mechanism is established. As a result, in most cases, instead of taking recourse to the Labour Court, the same conciliation and arbitration procedure is applied to settle disputes, and workers still suffer from the same investor bias problem. There is no legal scope for appeal against the decision of the arbitrators and conciliators. Despite the provision for invoking the jurisdiction of the common labour court, the workers often feel reluctant to bring their matters to this court. In the absence of a separate labour tribunal and the scope of appeal against arbitral award, the workers are being deprived of their right of access to justice, which leads to the deprivation of other rights such as minimum wages, appropriate working hours, leave, compensation and health care as guaranteed by the statutory laws.

Given this situation, the Bangladesh Legal Aid Service Trust (BLAST) lodged a writ petition with High Court Division of the Supreme Court of Bangladesh on public interest grounds. Based on this, the HCD issued a rule on 25 August 2008 requiring the government to explain why it should not be directed to form the labour tribunal and appellate tribunals in EPZs.[134] The government has not yet replied to the rule, and the tribunals have yet to be established.[135] Moreover, the government's position in this respect is made clear by the comment of the current labour minister in Bangladesh, who says he is unaware of the legal obligation to form labour tribunals in the EPZs.[136] So, implementing the legal principles regarding establishing a labour tribunal is a compelling need to protect fundamental labour rights, including other service interests, in all EPZs in Bangladesh.

The violation of labour and employment rights, including freedom of trade association and minimum wages, is frequent in the EPZs of Bangladesh. EPZs are the main base of foreign manufacturing and operate under a shield of exemption from applying labour laws dealing with rights related to employment security, trade unions and minimum wages. The enforcement mechanisms for limited rights, as introduced by the current applicable laws, are not adequate. Moreover, the judicial mechanism has not yet been set up as discussed earlier. The governmental laxity in regulating labour issues in EPZs is responsible for such a situation.

Given the discussion, it can be remarked that the existing mechanisms for enforcing labour standards do not work properly. They encounter many technical and non-technical legal barriers and inefficiency in their functions, including indulgence in corruption. As such, coordination between the government and stakeholders to improve labour standards is lacking. Despite huge resentment and dissatisfaction from the national and international community, the prolonging of such a situation testifies to the government's inertia in improving the regulatory framework in EPZs and non-EPZ investment locations in line with international standards. In addition, employers are still far from creating a compliance culture. In many cases, their compliance attempts are cosmetic, foreign-buyer-driven and not in the spirit of development by promoting labour rights. Foreign entrepreneurs take advantage of the weak labour regulation. The prevalent situation, therefore, requires bringing changes and improvement in the activities of existing enforcing authorities, such as restructuring the Department of labour, introducing a periodic monitoring system, establishing a full-time labour court with adequate staff and undertaking to establish the National Council for Occupation Health and Safety, bringing the EPZ workers under the application of enforcement mechanisms provided by the general labour laws.

5.6 Regulating Human Rights in Involuntary Resettlement

5.6.1 Constitutional Guarantees for Protection

It is already noted that most human rights issues affected by forced eviction are the loss of the right to ownership and property. The Constitution of Bangladesh acknowledges and guarantees the protection of people's ownership and property rights. Under Part 2 of its state policy, it recognises three kinds of ownership: public, cooperative and private.[137] It also recognises the right to property as the citizens' fundamental right. As for the protection of property rights, Article 42 of the Constitution provides that every citizen shall have the right to acquire, hold, transfer or otherwise dispose of property, and no property shall be compulsorily acquired, nationalised or requisitioned save by the authority of law.

This article also provides that any law made for this purpose shall (1) prescribe for the process of acquisition, holding and transfer of the property with compensation and (2) fix the compensation or specify the principles under which the compensation can be assessed or fixed, but no such law shall be called in question in any court on the ground that any provision in respect of such compensation is not adequate. The provision regarding the restriction to judicial recourse on the grounds of the inadequacy of compensation is opposed to the people's economic right to compensation in the case of involuntary resettlement. It nevertheless suggests the formulation of national legislation to establish a legal framework for regulating and protecting people's property rights that can apply to involuntary resettlement.

5.6.2 National Legislation

In Bangladesh, the principal legislation applicable for involuntary resettlement issues, particularly in the case of the loss of the right to land by the governmental acquisition or requisition for development purposes, is the *Acquisition and Requisition of Immovable Property Ordinance (ARIPO), 1982* (including all amendments up to 1994). Some other laws regulating the acquisition of immovable property include *the Land Acquisition Act of 1894, the Land Acquisition Act I of 1894, the Acquisition of Waste Land Act of 1950* and *the Chittagong Hill Tracts (Land Acquisition) Regulation.* The ARIPO has consolidated all previous legislation relating to the acquisition of immovable property. Hence, it becomes the sole legislation for the said purpose. It is notable that under the ARIPO, the acquisition or requisition right is vested only with the government for a public purpose, and the word public purpose, although not defined by the *Act* itself, covers in practice all kinds of development projects, extractive operations and manufacturing plants of MNCs on agreement with the government. This means, for example, that if the development or extractive project is a joint venture, the government acquires the property to implement the project for public purposes. If the project is funded, for example, with 100 per cent equity of a foreign or local company or by foreign or local individuals for any extractive or any development projects, the government acquires the property on behalf of the investing company or individual and transfers it to them based on the agreement between the government and the company or individual investors in an equal procedural manner applicable for public purpose. The associated issues of acquisition, such as taking possession and compensation of the displaced individuals, are determined on the basis of agreement in compliance with this law. The BEPZA makes the acquisition of land for an EPZ under the ARIPO 1982 under cover of public purpose.[138]

The question is how far this law considers the protection of people's right to their lands in the case of acquisition and requisition by the government for public purposes. It is understood by the discussion on state obligation under international human rights law as well as the policy directives of development agencies that for the effective protection of the rights of persons facing potential involuntary resettlement, the main focus of national legislation will be on some major essential requirements such as local consultation and consent requirements, an appropriate timeline for displacement, full information on resettlement measures and transitional support, compensation measures for resettlement and the right to access to legal protection against arbitrary displacement. This calls for evaluating the legal framework under ARIPO and other applicable special laws in Bangladesh to explore how far they maintain harmony with international standards to protect the relevant human rights of the people potentially affected by acquisition or requisition.

5.6.2.1 People's Consultation and Consent Requirements

Once a given investment project is under consideration, which requires the acquisition of lands and displacing the owners and others living at the site, it is widely recognised that the effective engagement of the local people through consultation and their consent is essential in the early stages of project design, not only to respect local rights but also to establish a company's social license to operate.[139] The international guidelines call for local consultation before investment approval including, *inter alia*, the *OECD Guidelines*, the *World Bank Guidelines* and the *UN Declaration on the Rights of Indigenous Peoples*.[140]

There is no provision requiring local people's consultation before the acquisition of land under ARIPO 1982. However, the consent of owners is taken differently. According to this, the Deputy Commissioner (DC), who is the executive authority for acquisition at the local level, serves a preliminary notice of acquisition at a convenient place or near the property stating that the property is proposed to be acquired.[141] Upon objection from the people interested in the property, the DC organises a hearing and then submits a report to the Government based on any objections for a final decision.[142] Then, the Government considers the report and makes a final decision.[143] This is the procedure for gaining the owners' "consent".

This procedure seems weak as it does not reflect on the representation of the community but only on the owners or settlers with a record of ownership.[144] It does not cover other potentially affected persons without a title or ownership record, such as informal settlers or squatters, occupiers and informal tenants or leaseholders. Although the objection right is conferred upon the person interested, the condition of ownership record refers only to owners and settlers with a record. In addition, this procedure does not follow the spirit and objective of recommendations under different international guidelines for consultation for free consent. The objective of the consultation is to share and communicate with the people about the purpose of acquisition and how and to what extent it serves the public interest. The procedure notification is not intended for the greater engagement of the interested people in the property. Therefore, notification of acquisition must be after consultation with the interested persons. Otherwise, their consent will never be free in a real sense.

Apart from ARIPO, for acquiring Indigenous land in the Hill Tracts of Bangladesh, according to the *District Council Act 1989*, the prior consent of the District Council is essential. There is no mention of the direct participation of any Indigenous landowner or how the District Council will gain the land from the original or customary owner. This legal provision contravenes the relocation directives by the *UN Declaration on the Rights of Indigenous Peoples*. Although the document lacks a binding status in the application, the prior or free and informed consent has been progressively interpreted in international human rights jurisprudence relating to the collective right to the property of Indigenous or tribal peoples. An example that is expedient in this context is an Indigenous land-grabbing case that occurred in the 1980s for mining for gas and oil. The seismic survey was launched by Shell, a multinational oil company, but was discontinued in the face of insurgency in the region. The survey was resumed in the 1990s by the US-registered company Union Oil Company of California (UNOCAL). An Arabian businessman later bought UNOCOL's interests. He began drilling for gas without reaching any understanding with the local Indigenous community leaders about the likely impact on inhabitants of the drilling sites and gas-line areas or the questions of dislocation, rehabilitation, compensation and so on.

5.6.2.2 Appropriate Schedule for Displacement

The general practice of setting an appropriate schedule for displacement is through consultation between the parties. According to the APRIO, the government begins action on acquisition after it decides to acquire certain lands for public purpose or public interest. The process starts with a notification and follow-up reply from the owners. Then, it proceeds step by step as per a prescribed time for the hearing of objections, if any, the government's final decision and settling matters relating to a compensation award. The acquisition is held after the payment of compensation, and thereafter, possession of the property will be taken officially through a declaration in the official gazette.[145] However, the law and practice are often inconsistent. For example, in the Jamuna Multipurpose Bridge (JMB) project, displacement occurred before compensation was completed.[146] There was no mention in the text of exactly when the displacement would commence.

5.6.2.3 Compensation Measure for Resettlement

Adequate compensation is a fundamental right in the case of deprivation of ownership caused by the acquisition or requisition of property. There is no specific provision in the *Hill Tracts Council Act 1989* about compensation in the case of the acquisition of property by the government. However, ARIPO 1982 sets out procedural and substantive principles relating to compensation for those deprived of their property as per the law. According to this Ordinance, upon the final decision of the government to acquire and take immediate possession of the property, the government DC will serve notice to all interested in the property to claim compensation.[147] After some necessary inquiries, the compensation will be awarded on a fixed date. It will be determined based on the market value of the property at the date of publication of the notice for acquisition.[148] In determining the amount of compensation, all incidental losses of the property owner or interested party caused by the acquisition will be taken into account and added to the property's value.[149] The important point in determining the amount is that if the acquisition is likely to compel the relocation of a residence or business place, then reasonable expenses incidental to such a change will be paid.[150]

The decision on compensation under the said legislation is entirely independent. It is not decided upon by prior agreement between the government and affected persons. Thus, in many cases, it creates chaotic situations and the deprivation of the affected persons' dues. There are displacement cases in the development projects in Bangladesh where the allotted compensation was inadequate. A survey study on the amount of compensation for displaced persons in land acquisition for the implementation of the JMB project in Bangladesh reveals that 77 per cent of affected respondents said that the amount of compensation was not sufficient at all against their losses.[151]

One reason for the inadequacy of compensation is that the Ordinance provides for compensation in cash according to market value. Cash compensation cannot substitute for the loss of land, particularly in the case of Indigenous people. There is a popular saying among the Havasupai Apache Indians in the US, a people displaced repeatedly by development projects: "Land is like diamond, but money is like ice".[152]

Under this Ordinance, there is a prominent legal gap regarding compensation eligibility. It considers a person who appears in the land administration records as an owner or person with legal title eligible for compensation. Therefore, temporary settlers or occupiers with no title or record are deprived of compensation. The ADB policy on involuntary resettlement suggests that the absence of formal legal title should not bar the giving of compensation.[153] The Ordinance determines compensation for lands and fixed assets,[154] but it lacks a provision requiring the assessment of the loss of income and livelihood.

5.6.2.4 Resettlement Measures, Transitional Support and Compensation Options

Proper resettlement measures for displaced persons are vital to protect fundamental rights to life. As inferred from human rights documents, the government is primarily responsible as the state authority. The government should design the resettlement plan with appropriate transitional support and budget allocation.[155] When involuntary resettlement becomes unavoidable, the government should inform the affected persons of its relocation plan and seek their options for compensation.[156] Under ARIPO, no provision creates an obligation for the government to take responsibility for the proper relocation arrangement, especially for those who lose their homesteads, which are their source or means of earning income. The law provides for incidental relocation costs, as mentioned earlier. However, it does not establish any provision to alleviate the long-term impact of forced displacement on people's livelihoods from the perspective of socio-economic rehabilitation.

In addition, legal consideration for determining compensation does not include options other than monetary compensation. Such a compensation method may create obstacles to economic and social rehabilitation. Option for compensation means the compensation should be determined based on the choice of the affected persons as they are not similar to the losses they sustain out of eviction. A survey study on the JMB project reveals that before resettlement, more than 72 per cent of people were engaged in agriculture. Still, the number of agricultural households decreased sharply, and now only 21 per cent are engaged in agriculture. Thus, the overall income status of these people who have no other alternative has decreased.[157]

5.7 The Enforcement of Legal Remedies

The ARIPO provides an arbitral system for the settlement of disputes about the acquisition of property by the government. The settlement of a dispute mainly involves an objection to the award of compensation and an objection to the acquisition of the property. Under this law, the DC is empowered on behalf of the government to acquire or requisite any private immovable property for public purposes or in the public interest, subject to maintaining certain procedural formalities and awarding compensation to the owners or persons interested in the property. When the person interested in the property raises an objection to or does not accept the award of compensation calculated by the DC against the given property, the dispute will be taken to an arbitral arrangement for settlement.[158] Upon the application of the interested person, the government will appoint a judicial officer, not below the rank of Sub-Judge, as an arbitrator to settle the matter in issue.[159] The arbitrator proceeds on the basis of the objection to award and will be guided by the principles relating to the determination of compensation as mentioned in sections 8, 9 or 20 of this *Ordinance*.

The Ordinance also provides for the constitution of the Arbitration Appellate Tribunal for appeal against the award of the arbitrator.[160] This tribunal comprises a person or persons who have been a district judge.[161] The decision of the Arbitration Appellate Tribunal is final. No further proceeding is allowed in this connection to a higher judiciary. The legal remedy for compensation is restricted to the arbitration system constituted by the government under this ordinance. The restriction for legal remedy for compensation to the arbitration system curtails the right of a person aggrieved to seek legal recourse to the highest judicial body where a similar pecuniary award for other grounds is entertained.

This Ordinance also guarantees the right of the object to the acquisition of the property when the formal notice is published for acquisition and the objection is entertained and decided by the Divisional Commissioner on behalf of the government. The decision of the Divisional Commissioner is final. No further scope for judicial remedy is available for the person aggrieved by the decision of the Divisional Commissioner under this Ordinance as it creates a bar to the jurisdiction of the court. Section 44 of the ARIPO states that no court shall entertain any suit or application against any order passed or any action taken under this Ordinance. Furthermore, no injunction shall be granted by any court in respect of any action to be taken in pursuance of any power conferred upon or under this Ordinance.

This judicial bar curtails the right to recourse judicial protection. It thus appears to be clearly at odds with the right conferred upon every citizen of Bangladesh under Article 44 of the Constitution of Bangladesh. This Article states that every person has the right to move to the HCD of the Supreme Court in the form of writ jurisdiction under Article 102 for the enforcement of fundamental rights recognised under part III of the Constitution. As mentioned earlier, the right to property protection is guaranteed fundamentally under this. In that sense, the underlying principle appears to be invalid by Article 26 (2) of the Constitution as it articulates that the State shall not make any law inconsistent with any provisions of this Part, and any law so made shall, to the extent of such inconsistency, be void.

In addition to a judicial bar, the principle of indemnification under this Ordinance restricts the scope of legal challenge by the aggrieved person in the case of the acquisition or requisition of his or her property. According to section 43, any act done in good faith under the cover of the power conferred by this law will not be liable to any suit, prosecution or legal proceeding. The point of justification seems to be that the act is done in good faith for the public purpose or public interest. However, the problem is that the term "public purpose or interest" is not defined by the law. Therefore, there is potential for the misinterpretation of this term and arbitrary practice by the administration to the advantage of such a principle. The absence of legal provisions requiring public participation in decision-making for acquisition broadens this scope.

5.8 Concluding Remarks

This chapter delves into the effectiveness of laws and policies in Bangladesh in protecting the rights of individuals affected by foreign investment in manufacturing, development projects, and mining, focusing on labour rights and the rights of individuals forced to relocate from their homes. The primary goal was to enhance the protection of people's rights by ensuring compliance by foreign companies and strengthening laws, if necessary.

The existing laws do not hold foreign companies accountable for upholding people's rights. Attention to people's rights only gained momentum after 2009, and the regulations do not cover all issues impacted by foreign investment. Additionally, there are disparities in the protection of labour rights for workers in different regions, with some workers not being granted the full extent of their rights to join groups, discuss wages, receive fair pay or be treated equally in the workplace. Furthermore, national laws do not measure up to the standards of other countries in terms of allowing workers to join groups, discussing wages, preventing forced labour and ensuring equal treatment in the workplace. Although workplace safety regulations seem comprehensive, they fail to meet international standards. There are also challenges concerning compliance with the rules and oversight by regulatory bodies. Finally, there are no specific regulations or plans to safeguard the rights of individuals forced to relocate due to development projects and mining, and the existing regulations do not provide adequate assistance in line with international standards. The existing laws concerning foreign businesses and labour regulations in Bangladesh do not effectively address the rights of individuals. This highlights the urgent need for substantial changes, whether through modifying current laws or creating new ones, to ensure the protection of people's rights in the workplace and in relation to foreign investment.

Notes

1 See UNRISD, *States of Disarray: The Social Effect of Globalization* (Executive Summary of an UNRISD Report for the World Summit for Social Development, 1995) UN, Geneva <www.unrisd.org/8 0256B3C005BCCF9/.../$file/Statesof Dis_ES.pdf> 30 April 2024; see Peter Stalker, *States of Disarray: The Social Effects of Globalization* (Diane Publishing, 1998) <books.google.com/books/a bout/states_of_Disarray.htm?id> 30 April 2024; see also UNRISD, *Visible Hands: Taking Responsibility for Social Development* (2000) <www.unrisd.org/.../FE969439D82 B52480256B670065EFA1?> 30 April 2024.

2 Shyami Fernando Puvimanasinghe, *Foreign Investment Human Rights and the Environment: A Perspective from South Asia on the Role of Public International Law for Development* (Martinus Nijhoff Publishers, 2007) 1; MR Anderson, 'Litigation and Activism: The Bhopal Case' (1993) 12 *Third World Legal Studies* 177, 179; CM Abraham and Shusila Abraham, 'The Bhopal Case and the Development of Environmental Law in India' (1991) 40(2) *The International and Comparative Law Quarterly* 334.

3 See the UN Commission on Human Rights, *Forced Evictions* (CHR Res. 1993/77 (1)). <http://www.ohchr.org/EN/Issues/Housing/Pages/ForcedEvictions.aspx> 30 April 2024.

4 See Adam McBeth, 'The Shift towards Emerging Economy Financing of Development Projects: Implications for Human Rights Standards' in Rowena Maguire, Bridget Lewis and Charles Sampford (eds) *Shifting Global Powers and International Law: Challenges and Opportunities* (Routledge, 2013) 228, 229.

5 See Adam McBeth, 'The Shift towards Emerging Economy Financing of Development Projects: Implications for Human Rights Standards' in Rowena Maguire, Bridget Lewis and Charles Sampford (eds) *Shifting Global Powers and International Law: Challenges and Opportunities* (Routledge, 2013) 228, 229.

6 See 'Doing Business in Difficult Places', *The Economist*, 20 May 2000, 127.

7 See 'Doing Business in Difficult Places', *The Economist*, 20 May 2000, 127.

8 PT Muchlinski, 'Human Rights and Multinationals: Is There a Problem?' (2001) 77 *International Affairs* 31, 44.

9 For example, in the *Doe v Unocal* case, the litigants brought claims under the ATCA against US-based oil company Unocal for egregious human rights violations committed by the Burmese military in connection with the construction of the Yadana pipeline from Burma to Thailand. Allegedly, Burmese army units were hired to secure and protect the project.

10 For example, in the *DOE v Unocal* case, the litigants brought a claim under the ATCA against the US-based oil company Unocal for egregious human rights violations committed by the Burmese military in connection with the construction of the Yadana pipeline from Burma to Thailand. Allegedly, Burmese Army units were hired to secure and protect the project.

11 Article 34 states "all forms of forced labour are prohibited and any contravention of this provision shall be an offence punishable in accordance with law".

12 Article 28 states "the State shall not discriminate against any citizens on grounds only of religion, race, caste, sex and place of birth".

13 Article 29 states "there shall be equality of opportunity for all citizens in respect of employment or office in the service of the Republic".

14 Article 38 states "every citizen shall have the right to form associations or unions, subject to any reasonable restrictions imposed by law in the interests of morality and public order".

15 Article 42 of the notes that "subject to any restriction imposed by law, every citizen shall have the right to acquire, hold, transfer or otherwise dispose of property, and no property shall be compulsorily acquired, nationalised or requisitioned save by authority of law".

16 It is noted that before the adoption of the *Labour Act of 2006*, there were about 46 laws in force in Bangladesh encompassing labour and industrial sectors. After the enactment of the *Labour Act*, 25 of the prevailing enactments stood repealed and were amalgamated with the new Code. The laws are *the Workmen's Compensation Act, 1923* (VIII of 1923); *the Children (Pledging of Labour) Act, 1933*; *the Workmen's Protection Act, 1934* (IV of 1935); *the Doc Labourers Act, 1934* (XIX of 1934); *the Payment of Wages Act, 1936* (IV of 1936); *the Employer's Liability Act, 1938* (XXVI of 1938); *the Employment of Children Act, 1*038 (XXVI of 1938); *the Maternity Benefit Act, 1941* (XIX of 1941); *the Motor Vehicles (Drivers) Ordinance, 1942* (V of 1942); *the Maternity Benefit (Tea Estate) Act, 1950* (XX of 1950); *the Employment (Records of Service) Act, 1951*; *the Bangladesh Plantation Employees Provident Fund Ordinance, 1959* (XXXI of 1959); *the Coal Mines (Fixation of Rates of Wages) Ordinance, 1960* (XXXIX of 1960); *the Road Transport Workers Ordinance, 1961* (XXVII of 1961); *the Minimum Wages Ordinance 1961* (XXXIV of 1961); *the Plantation Labour Ordinance, 1962* (XXIX of 1962); *the Apprenticeship Ordinance, 1962* (LVI of 1962); *the Factories Act, 1965* (IV of 1956); *the Shops and Establishment Act, 1965* (VII of 1965); *the Employment of Labour (Standing Orders) Act, 1965* (VIII of 1965); *the Companies Profits (Workers Participation) Act, 1968* (XII of 1968); *the Industrial Relations Ordinance, 1969* (XXII of 1969); *the Newspaper Employees (Conditions of Service) Act, 1974* (XXX of 1974); *and the Dock Worker (Regulation and Employment) Act, 1980* (XVII of 1980).

17 *Bangladesh Labour Act 2006* (Bangladesh) s. 4(2) (Lxi).

18 *Bangladesh Labour Act 2006* (Bangladesh) s. 4(2) (Lli).

19 The eight fundamental conventions are the *Freedom of Association and Protection of Right to Organize 1948*, *Right to Organize and Collective Bargaining 1949*, *Forced Labour 1930*, *Abolition of Forced Labour 1957*, *Equal Remuneration 1951*, *Discrimination (Employment and Occupation) 1958*, *Minimum Age 1973* and the *Worst Forms of Child Labour 1999*.

20 See International Labour Office, *Decent Work Country Programme Bangladesh* (2006–2009) <http://www.ilo.org> 30 April 2024.

21 See *International Covenant on Civil and Political Rights*, 1966 (United Nations) art. 8 <http//www.treaties.un.org/doc/Publication/UNTS/.../volume-999-I-14668-English.p> 30 April 2024.
22 See *International Covenant on Civil and Political Rights*, 1966 (United Nations) art. 22.
23 See *International Covenant on Economic, Social and Cultural Rights* (United Nations) 1966, arts. 6, 7, 8 and 12.
24 See *the Bangladesh Labour Act 2006* (Bangladesh) s. 176.
25 See *ILO Convention 87 on Freedom of Association and Protection of the Right to Organise*, 1948, art. 2.
26 See *ILO Convention 87 on Freedom of Association and Protection of the Right to Organise*, 1948, art. 3.
27 See *ILO Convention 87 on Freedom of Association and Protection of the Right to Organise*, 1948, art 4.
28 See *the Bangladesh Labour Act 2006* (Bangladesh) sec. 176 (a), (c) and (d).
29 See *the Bangladesh Labour Act 2006* (Bangladesh) ss. 179 and 182.
30 See *the Bangladesh Labour Act 2006* (Bangladesh) s. 179(2).
31 Previous legislations, the Factory Act 1965 and Industrial Relations Ordinance 1969, dealt with the issue of trade unionization, which were repealed by the enactment of the BLA 2006. See Abdullah Al Faruque, *Current Status and Evolution of Industrial Relations System in Bangladesh* (International Labour Organization, 2009) 12.
32 Previous legislations, the Factory Act 1965 and Industrial Relations Ordinance 1969, dealt with the issue of trade unionization, which were repealed by the enactment of the BLA 2006. See Abdullah Al Faruque, *Current Status and Evolution of Industrial Relations System in Bangladesh* (International Labour Organization, 2009) 12.
33 Previous legislations, the Factory Act 1965 and Industrial Relations Ordinance 1969, dealt with the issue of trade unionization, which were repealed by the enactment of the BLA 2006. See Abdullah Al Faruque, *Current Status and Evolution of Industrial Relations System in Bangladesh* (International Labour Organization, 2009) 12.
34 Hisham Bin Mustofa, 'Amended *Bangladesh Labour Act 2013* under criticism', *Priyo News* (online), 22 July 2013 <http://news.priyo.com/2013/07/22/amemded-bangladesh-labour-act-2013-under-critics....> 30 April 2024.
35 See the Danish Trade Union Development Agency, Labour Market Profile Bangladesh (2024/2025) <https://www. ulandsecretariate.dk> 24 June 2024.
36 See the Danish Trade Union Development Agency, Labour Market Profile Bangladesh (2024/2025) <https://www. ulandsecretariate.dk> 24 June 2024.
37 The *Bangladesh Labour Act 2006* (Bangladesh) s. 205.
38 The *Bangladesh Labour Act 2006* (Bangladesh) s. 206(1).
39 Faruque, above n 31, 23.
40 International Trade Union Confederation, *Bangladesh-ITUC Survey of Violations of Trade Union Rights* (2013) <survey.ituc-csi.org/Bangladesh.htm> 30 April 2024.
41 *The Bangladesh Export Processing Zones Act 1980 as amended in 1984* (Bangladesh) s. 11A.
42 These two labour laws are presently repealed and amalgamated with the current *Bangladesh Labour Act 2006.*
43 See Ramapriya Gopalakrishna, 'Freedom of Association and Collective Bargaining in Export Processing Zones: Role of the ILO Supervisory Mechanisms' (Working Paper No.1, International Labour Office, 2007) <www.ilo.org/wcmsp5/groups/public/---ed.../wcms_087917.pdf> 30 April 2024.
44 See Ramapriya Gopalakrishna, 'Freedom of Association and Collective Bargaining in Export Processing Zones: Role of the ILO Supervisory Mechanisms' (Working Paper No.1, International Labour Office, 2007) <www.ilo.org/wcmsp5/groups/public/---ed.../wcms_087917.pdf> 30 April 2024.
45 See Export Promotion Bureau, *Bangladesh EPZ* (2007) <http://www.epb.gov.bd/bangladesh_epz.htm> 30 April 2024.

46 M Abu Eusuf, ABM Omor Faruque and Attiur Rahman, 'Institutions for Facilitating FDI: Issues for BEPZA, Bangladesh' (Briefing Paper No. 10, IPPG and CUTS International) <www.ippg.org.uk> 30 April 2024.
47 M Abu Eusuf, ABM Omor Faruque and Attiur Rahman, 'Institutions for Facilitating FDI: Issues for BEPZA, Bangladesh' (Briefing Paper No. 10, IPPG and CUTS International) <www.ippg.org.uk> 30 April 2024.
48 See *the EPZ Workers Associations and Industrial Relations Act 2004* (Bangladesh) s. 5.
49 See *the EPZ Workers Associations and Industrial Relations Act 2004* (Bangladesh) s. 24.
50 See *the EPZ Workers Associations and Industrial Relations Act 2004* (Bangladesh) s. 25(1).
51 See *the EPZ Workers Associations and Industrial Relations Act 2004* (Bangladesh) s. 88(1).
52 Such as the contravention of any of the provisions of association's constitution; see *the EPZ Workers Associations and Industrial Relations Act 2004* (Bangladesh) ss. 36(1) (c), (e),–(h) and 42(1) (a).
53 See *the EPZ Workers Associations and Industrial Relations Act 2004* (Bangladesh) ss. 5 (6) and (7), 28 (1), 29 and 32 (4).
54 International Labour Organization, *Report on the Committee on Freedom of Association* (Report no. 357, ILO, 2010) <http://www.ilo.org> 30 April 2024.
55 See *ILO Tripartite Declaration of Principles Concerning Multinational Enterprises and Social Policy* 1977 (3rd. ed., 2001), para 46.
56 See ILO, *Report of the Committee of Experts on the Application of Conventions and Recommendation* (Part IIIA, 2010) <http://www.ilo.org> 30 April 2024.
57 See *the EPZ Workers' Welfare Organization and Industrial Relations Act, 2010* (Bangladesh) s. 5.
58 See *the EPZ Workers' Welfare Organization and Industrial Relations Act, 2010* (Bangladesh) s. 80.
59 See *the EPZ Workers' Welfare Organization and Industrial Relations Act, 2010* (Bangladesh) s. 7.
60 See *the EPZ Workers' Welfare Organization and Industrial Relations Act, 2010* (Bangladesh) s. 37(2).
61 Gopalakrishna, above n 44.
62 The convention is titled '*ILO Convention Concerning the Prohibition and Immediate Action for the Elimination of Worst Form of Child Labour' (No. 182), 1999.* It came into force in 2000.
63 See the Preamble of the *ILO Convention 182.*
64 See *the Bangladesh Labour Act 2006* (Bangladesh) s. 44.
65 ITUC, *Internationally Recognised Core Labour Standards in Bangladesh* (Report for the WTO General Council Review of the Trade Policies of Bangladesh, Geneva, 24 and 26 September, 2012) <www.ituc-csi.org/IMG/pdf/bangladesh-final.pdf> 5 May 2024. The ILO estimates that there are seven million child workers in Bangladesh, of whom 1.3 million are engaged in hazardous work. Children work mostly in agriculture, manufacturing and services, including domestic service and street-based activities.
66 *The Bangladesh Labour Act* 2006 (Bangladesh) s. 35. The term legal guardian includes any person having legal custody of or control over a child.
67 See Ritesh Sarna, *The Impact of Core Labour Standards on FDI in East Asia* (2005) The Japan Institute for Labour Policy and Training, Tokyo <www.jil.go.jp/profile/documents/sarna/pdf> 5 May 2024; David Kucera, 'The Effects of Core Worker Rights on Labour Costs and Foreign Direct Investment: Evaluating the "Conventional Wisdom"' (Discussion Paper, 130/2001, Decent Work Research Programme, International Institute for Labour Studies) <https://www.ilo.org/inst> 5 May 2024, 59–60; see also OECD, *Foreign Direct Investment for Development: Maximising Benefits, Minimising Costs* (2002) OECD <http://www.oecd.org> 5 May 2024.

68 *The ILO Discrimination (Employment and Occupation) Convention* (1958) art. 1 (1)(a).
69 *The ILO Discrimination (Employment and Occupation) Convention* (1958) art. 1 (1).
70 It means, for example, any firm or industry may hire a skilled worker at a higher salary, or a distinction is allowed on the basis of the nature of the work.
71 *The ILO Discrimination (Employment and Occupation) Convention* (1958) art. 1 (2).
72 The Equal Remuneration Convention (1951) art. 1 (b).
73 See the *ILO Declaration on Fundamental Principles and Rights at Work* (1998), art. 2 (d).
74 See the *ILO Declaration on Fundamental Principles and Rights at Work* (1998), art. 2.
75 See the *Constitution of the People's Republic of Bangladesh 1972*, art. 29 (1), (2).
76 See the *Labour Code of Socialist Republic of Vietnam*, 1994 (Vietnam) art. 5.
77 It is stated that in determining wages for any worker, the principle of equal wages for male or female workers for work of equal nature or value shall be followed and no discrimination shall be made in this respect on the ground of sex.
78 See *Bangladesh Labour Act 2006* (Bangladesh) s. 329.
79 Stephan Klasen, *Does Gender Inequality Reduce Growth and Development: Evidence from Cross-Country Regressions*? (Policy Research Report on Gender and Development, Working Paper Series No. 7, World Bank, November 1999) The World Bank Development Research Group <http://www.worldbank.org/gender/prr> 5 May 2024.
80 M Sornarajah, *The International Law on Foreign Investment* (Cambridge, 3rd ed., 2010) 114.
81 M Sornarajah, *The International Law on Foreign Investment* (Cambridge, 3rd ed., 2010) 114. The World Bank, *Engendering Development: Through Gender Equality in Rights, Resources and Voice* (A Policy Research Paper, World Bank, 2001) <http://documents. worldbank.org> 5 May 2024.
82 M Sornarajah, *The International Law on Foreign Investment* (Cambridge, 3rd ed., 2010) 114. The World Bank, *Engendering Development: Through Gender Equality in Rights, Resources and Voice* (A Policy Research Paper, World Bank, 2001) <http://documents. worldbank.org> 5 May 2024.
83 See *the Forced Labour Convention* (1930) art. 2(1).
84 See *the Abolition of Forced Labour Convention* (1957) art. 1(b).
85 See Sornarajah, above n 81, 114; See also Megun Juan, Jesus Campo and Patricia Campo, 'The Accountability of Multinational Corporations for Human Rights Violations' (2010) 64/65 *Cuadernos Constitucionales de la Cátedra Fadrique Furió Ceriol* 171, 180; Lillian Manzella, Julieta Rossi and Nichlas Lusiani, *Collective Report on Business and Human Rights* (June 2008) International Network for Economic, Social and Cultural Rights <http://www.escr-net.org/ usr_doc/BHRCollectiveReport_ESCR-Net.pdf> 5 May 2024.
86 *The Bangladesh Labour Act 2006* (Bangladesh) s. 37.
87 *The Penal Code 1860* (Bangladesh) s. 374.
88 See *Universal Declaration of Human Rights* (1948) art. 23(2), (3); *International Covenant on Economic, Social and Cultural Rights* (1966) art. 7(a), (b), (d).
89 See *ILO's Minimum Wage Fixing Convention* (1970) art. 3(a), (b).
90 See *ILO's Minimum Wage Fixing Convention* (1970) art. 4.
91 It is noteworthy that the payment and protection of wages and other related matters were previously regulated by the *Payment of Wages Act 1936*. This Act had a wide coverage. The workers employed in factories, shops, industrial and commercial establishments such as road transport services, railways, dock, jetties, inland steam vessels, mine, oil fields, plantations or any other workshop have been brought within the purview of this legislation. This law has now been merged with the newly introduced *Bangladesh Labour Act* 2006.
92 *The Bangladesh Labour Act 2006* (Bangladesh) s. 149 (1).
93 *The Bangladesh Labour Act 2006* (Bangladesh) s. 139.
94 *The Bangladesh Labour Act 2006* (Bangladesh) s.141.

95 See *Minimum Wage Fixing Convention* (1970) s. 3.

96 Article 3(a) and 3(b) of the *Minimum Wage Fixing Convention* 1970 states that elements to be taken into consideration in determining the level of minimum wages shall, so far as possible and appropriate to national practice and conditions, include: (a) the needs of workers and their families, taking into account the general level of wages in the country, the cost of living, social security benefits and the relative living standards of other social groups; (b) economic factors, including the requirements of economic development, levels of productivity and the desirability of attaining and maintaining a high level of employment.

97 *The Bangladesh Labour Act 2006* (Bangladesh) s. 140.

98 *The Bangladesh Labour Act 2006* (Bangladesh) s. 142.

99 See *the Bangladesh Gazette (Extra Ordinary Issue)*, S.R.O. No. 301 (2006, 2014 and 2023) <http://www.Ain/2006/ SROKOM/Sha-6/Ni.Mo.Board-1/2006> 5 May 2024.

100 *The Bangladesh Labour Act 2006* (Bangladesh) s. 142.

101 Faruque, above n 31.

102 *Instruction No. 2 of Bangladesh Export Processing Zones Authority 1980*, part 1.

103 *Instruction No. 2 of Bangladesh Export Processing Zones Authority 1980*, part 1.

104 *Instruction No. 2 of Bangladesh Export Processing Zones Authority 1980*, part 5; see also Bangladesh Export Processing Zones Authority, *Re-fixing of Minimum Wages and Benefits for the Workers of the Enterprise of EPZs* (October 2010) <www.epzbangladesh.org.bd> 5 May 2024.

105 See Abdullah Siddiqui, *Bangladesh: Human Rights in Export Processing Zones* (2007) Asia Monitor Resource Centre <http://www.amrc.org.hk/alu_article/ export_processing_zones/ bangladesh_human _rights...> 5 May 2024.

106 See Bangladesh Export Processing Zones Authority, *Re-fixing of Minimum Wages and Benefits for the Workers of the Enterprise of EPZs* (October 2010) <www.epz bangladesh.org.bd> 5 May 2024.

107 See Sadrel Reza, M Ali Rashid and AHM Mabubul Alam, *Private Foreign Investment in Bangladesh* (University Press Limited, Bangladesh, 1987) 87.

108 See Debaprya Bhattacharya, *Export Processing Zones in Bangladesh: Economic Impact and Social Issues* (International Labour Organisation, 1998) 33.

109 See, for example, B Aitken, A Harrison and R Lipsey, 'Wages and Foreign Ownership: A Comparative Study of Mexico, Venezuela, and the United States' (1996) 40 *Journal of International Economics*, 345, 371; D Velde and O Morrissey, 'Do Workers in Africa Get a Wage Premium if Employed in Firms Owned by Foreigners?' (2003) 12 *Journal of African Economies*, 41–73; D Brown, A Deardoff and R Stern, *The Effects of Multinational Production on Wages and Working Conditions in Developing Countries* (Research Working Paper 9669, National Bureau of Economic Research, 2003).

110 See Pedro S Martins, 'Do Foreign Firms Really Pay Higher Wages? Evidence from Different Estimators' (Discussion Paper Series, No. 1388, Institute for the Study of Labour, November 2004) <http://ftp.iza.org/dp1388.pdf> 5 May 2024.

111 For a case summary, see Richard Meeran, 'The Unveiling of Transnational Corporations: A Direct Approach' in Michael Addo (ed.) *Human Rights and the Responsibility of Transnational Corporations* (Kluwer Law International, Hague, 1st ed. 1999) 161–170; see Marion Weschka, 'Human Rights and Multinational Enterprises: How Can Multinational Enterprises Be Held for Human Rights Violations Committed Abroad?' (2006) 66 Zeitschrift fur Auslandisches Offentlisches Recht und Volkerrecht (Zoa RV), 631.

112 *The Bangladesh Labour Act 2006* (Bangladesh) chapter 5.

113 See the facts of the cases of *Thor Chemical Holding Ltd., RTZ Corp. Plc* ([1995] TLR 579), and *Cape Plc.* ([1996] Q.B 361).

114 For example, major ILO Instruments concerning safety and health are the *Protection of Workers' Health Recommendation, 1953 (No. 97), Occupational Safety*

and Health Convention (No. 155) and Recommendation (No. 164), 1981, Occupational Health Services Convention (No. 161) and Recommendation (No. 171), 1993, Prevention of Major Industrial Accident Convention (No. 174) and Recommendation (No. 181), 1993, List of Occupational Diseases Recommendation, 2002 (No. 174), Protocol of 2002 to the Occupational Safety and Health Convention, 1981 (No. 155) and *the Promotional Framework for Occupational Safety and Health Convention (No. 187), 2006 and Recommendation (No. 197), 2006.*

115 *The ILO Tripartite Declaration of Principles Concerning Multinational Enterprises and Social Policy* (1977, 3rd ed., 2001) paragraph 37.

116 See *the Bangladesh Labour Act 2006* (Bangladesh) ss. 5–60.

117 See *the Bangladesh Labour Act 2006* (Bangladesh) ss. 61–78.

118 See *the Bangladesh Labour Act 2006* (Bangladesh) ss. 79–88.

119 See *the Bangladesh Labour Act 2006* (Bangladesh) s. 88.

120 See *the Mines Act, 1923* (Bangladesh) ss. 17 to 22.

121 See William Gomes, 'Reason and Responsibility: The Rana Plaza Collapse' *Open Democracy* (online), 9 May 2013 <http://www.opendemocracy.net/opensecurity/william-gomes/reason-and-responsibility-rana-plaza-collapse> 10 May 2024.

122 For details, see Syed Jamal Uddin, 'The Fallout from the *Tazreen* fire', *The Financial Express*, 29 November 2012; Asia Monitor Resource Centre, *Tazreen Fire -The Ground Realities* (Tazreen Incident Investigation Report, 2012) <http://www.amrc.org.hk/system/files/Tazreen%20Report.pdf> 10 May 2024.

123 See *the Bangladesh Labour Act 2006* (Bangladesh) s. 317 (1).

124 See *the Bangladesh Labour Act 2006* (Bangladesh) s. 317 (4).

125 For instance, imposition of any condition in a contract of employment restraining the right to joining or continuing in a trade union; refusal to employ on the ground of trade; discriminating against any person in the employment, promotion, condition of employment on the ground of trade union membership; dismissal, discharge, removal from employment on the ground of trade union and so on.

126 *The Bangladesh Labour Act 2006* (Bangladesh), s. 318.

127 *The Bangladesh Labour Act 2006* (Bangladesh), s. 319.

128 *The Bangladesh Labour Act 2006* (Bangladesh), s. 323 (2).

129 *The Bangladesh Labour Act 2006* (Bangladesh), s. 323 (5).

130 *The Bangladesh Labour Act 2006* (Bangladesh), s. 214 (10).

131 *The Bangladesh Labour Act 2006* (Bangladesh), s. 213.

132 *The Bangladesh Labour Act 2006* (Bangladesh) s. 33(1) (2).

133 See Faruque, above n 31.

134 See *the Constitution of the Peoples' Republic of Bangladesh* 1972, art. 102.

135 See Bangladesh Export Processing Zones Authority, *Instruction No.1 of* 1989, s. 29.

136 *The EPZ Workers' Association and Industrial Relations Act,* 2004 (Bangladesh) s. 56.

137 *The EPZ Workers Welfare Association and Industrial Relations Act,* 2010 (Bangladesh) s. 48 and 52.

138 Faruque, above n 32.

139 *BLAST and Another vs Bangladesh and Others [Labour Tribunal Case] (2008) Writ Petition No. 6448.*

140 Special Reporter, 'Two Vital Tribunals Yet to Be Set up in the Country's EPZs', *The Financial Express* (Dhaka, Bangladesh), 14 November 2013 <http://www.thefinancialexpress-bd.com /2013/11/14/3881> 20 May 2024.

141 Special Reporter, 'Two Vital Tribunals Yet to Be Set up in the Country's EPZs', *The Financial Express* (Dhaka, Bangladesh), 14 November 2013 <http://www.thefinancialexpress-bd.com /2013/11/14/3881> 20 May 2024.

142 The *Constitution of Peoples' Republic of Bangladesh* 1972, art. 13.

143 See *the Bangladesh Private Export Processing Zones Authority Act 1996* (Bangladesh), s. 12.

144 Lorenzo Cotula, *Foreign Investment, Law and Sustainable Development: A Handbook on Agriculture and Extractive Industries* (International Institute for Environment and Development, 2014) 97.
145 See OECD Guidelines, which require community participation and integration with the host population; Article 10 of the UN Declaration on the Rights of Indigenous Peoples (2007) requires the free and prior consent of Indigenous people for relocation.
146 *The Acquisition and Requisition of Immovable Property Ordinance* 1982 (Bangladesh) s. 3.
147 *The Acquisition and Requisition of Immovable Property Ordinance* 1982 (Bangladesh) s. 4(1) (2) (3).
148 *The Acquisition and Requisition of Immovable Property Ordinance* 1982 (Bangladesh) s. 5.
149 *The Acquisition and Requisition of Immovable Property Ordinance* 1982 (Bangladesh) s. 4(3).
150 *The Acquisition and Requisition of Immovable Property Ordinance* 1982 (Bangladesh) s. 11(1).
151 Syed Al Atahar, 'Development Project, Land Acquisition and Resettlement in Bangladesh: A Quest for Well Formulated National Resettlement and Rehabilitation Policy' (2013) 3(7) *International Journal of Humanities and Social Science* 306, 313.
152 *The Acquisition and Requisition of Immovable Property Ordinance* 1982 (Bangladesh) s. 6.
153 *The Acquisition and Requisition of Immovable Property Ordinance* 1982 (Bangladesh) s. 8.
154 *The Acquisition and Requisition of Immovable Property Ordinance* 1982 (Bangladesh) s. 8 (b), (c), (d).
155 *The Acquisition and Requisition of Immovable Property Ordinance* 1982 (Bangladesh) s. 8 (e).
156 Al Atahar, above n 151, 312.
157 Scott Guggenheim, 'Development and the Dynamics of Displacement' (a paper presented for Workshop on Rehabilitation of Displaced Persons, Institute for Social and Economic Change and MYRADA, Bangalore, India, 1990) 20.
158 <http://scholar.google.com.au/scholar?hl=en&q=development+and+the+dynamics+of+displacement&btnG=&as_sdt=1%2C5&as_sdtp=2> 20 May 2024; MQ Zaman, *Land Acquisition and Compensation in Involuntary Resettlement*, Cultural Survival <http://www.culturalsurvival.org/.../land-acquisition-and-compensation-involunt> 20 May 2024.
159 See *ADB Safe Policy on Involuntary Resettlement* (2009) para 34.
160 *The Acquisition and Reacquisition of Immovable Property Ordinance 1982* (Bangladesh) 8 (b). Clause B includes the loss of trees and crops in the compensation amount.
161 See Committee on Economic Social and Cultural Rights, *The Right to Adequate Housing: Forced Evictions*, UN Doc. E/1998/22 (20 May 1997) annex IV (General Comment 7) 15.

6 Protecting FDI and National Interest

6.1 Introduction

Investment protection is the central concern of foreign investors in host states. The legal security afforded by the host state's national legislations or their bilateral agreement allows them to exercise the economic freedom they desire while investing in a foreign country. The legal protection of investment property is instrumental in motivating foreign firms to pursue new investments and ensures a profitable outcome. Investors are less likely to invest in countries that do not provide legal safeguards for their investment properties or where chances are meagre to maximise business profits. Given this tendency, the host state's national laws and bilateral treaties are substantially influenced by and geared towards guaranteeing investment protection. Therefore, it is often seen that foreign direct investment (FDI) laws, particularly bilateral treaties, are qualified with the words "Promotion and Protection".[1]

Several issues may require legal protection in investment, but two issues, protection against expropriation and protection through dispute settlement, are prominently guaranteed through FDI legislation and bilateral treaties. The expropriation of property was once a major concern of foreign investors, especially when the communist regimes were active and the concept of absolute sovereignty more or less influenced countries. The rapid acceptance of economic globalisation and the demise of communism contributed to the alarming rise in unilateral declarations of protection against expropriation through national legislation. The expropriation issue was also prominently placed in the bilateral investment treaties (BITs). In addition, in choosing a means of dispute settlement, although different options are made through BIT negotiations, international arbitral settlement has become the most preferred means of settlement.

Legislative or agreement-based guarantees for lawful treatment concerning expropriation remove what foreign investors fear to be the greatest threat to their investments, as expropriation is the severest form of a host state's interference with the property involved in an investment. Investors are hesitant to invest where there is a danger of expropriation of physical assets. Similarly,

DOI: 10.4324/9781003469117-6

legal guarantees for dispute settlement in the host state provide hope for a remedy in the event of government intervention and for the enforcement of an investment contract in a neutral way. As the rise of FDI inflow is deemed dependent upon the availability of strong protection against expropriation and dispute settlement on the part of host countries, the protection regime usually develops to the gratification of foreign investors or capital exporting countries at the compromise of the host state's national interest. As a result, some important economic and social development issues remain inarticulate or unaddressed in the legal regimes of host states, such as determining compensation for expropriation, expropriation for the national development interest, exhausting of local remedies in dispute settlements and the inclusion of non-economic development issues.

6.2 The Protection against Expropriation of Investment

6.2.1 Constitutional Guarantee

In Bangladesh, the constitutional guarantee for protection against expropriation is recognised only as a citizen's fundamental right; it does not extend to foreign investment, and thus, there is no explicit guarantee for the protection of foreign investment. Article 42 of the *Constitution of Bangladesh* states that subject to any restrictions imposed by law, every citizen shall have the right to acquire, hold, transfer or otherwise dispose of property, and no property shall be compulsorily acquired, nationalised, or requisitioned save by the authority of law. The constitutional words reflect the prohibition of arbitrary and forced expropriation applicable to the citizens only.

Foreign investors cannot obtain citizenship automatically in Bangladesh unless the threshold investment amount is equivalent to US$500,000 or by transferring US$1,000,000 to any recognised financial institution (non-repatriable).[2]

Some constitutional provisions relating to expropriation remain general and non-qualified. The *Constitution of the Republic of Croatia* is one such provision, which states that property may be restricted and expropriated by law in the interest of the Republic of Croatia.[3] So, in order to establish a constitutional guarantee explicitly for the right of protection against expropriation applicable to all, the word "every citizen" should be replaced by "every person" or "every individual".

6.2.2 Statutory Guarantee

Although the *Constitution of Bangladesh* lacks any specific guarantee for the protection of foreign investment against expropriation, this is recognised by the Foreign Private Investment (Promotion and Protection) Act (FPIA) 1980.

It is also recognised in BITs between Bangladesh and others, supplementing the existing law. Section 7 of the FPIA establishes the substantive principle regarding expropriation by stating that "foreign private investment shall not be expropriated or nationalised or be subject to any measures having the effect of expropriation or nationalisation except for public purpose against adequate compensation which shall be paid expeditiously and freely transferable". The wording of the section reflects on the ambit of prohibition and the conditions under which the expropriation is permitted, which means the legality and illegality of expropriation. The ambit of the prohibition covers both direct and indirect expropriation without public purpose and compensation. On the other hand, expropriation is legal if it is done for the public's benefit and with compensation. This wording of the principles simultaneously expresses the right of investors to be protected against expropriation and the right of the host to expropriate under prescribed circumstances. Under this section, the legality or illegality test contains four basic legal elements: direct and indirect expropriation, public purpose and adequate compensation, as conditions that require some clarification. There is no mention of non-discrimination and due process as conditions. However, internationally recognised requirements are often seen to be negotiated through BITs in Bangladesh.[4]

6.2.2.1 Direct Expropriation

While there is no definition of expropriation in the text of the *FPIA 1980*, the formal phrase "expropriation or nationalisation" in the context of prohibition reflects the meaning of direct expropriation. These two terms are often used interchangeably in the FDI legislation and BITs. Confiscation also has a similar meaning, but it is not used in modern texts. In practice, it refers to the direct transfer of private-owned property partly or in full to the state ownership or ownership of the third party with government interference. It may also refer to the formal transfer of title or outright physical seizure, or obligatory transfer of title in favour of the host state and capricious confiscation.[5] It means the deprivation of ownership takes place overtly and permanently. Determining any act as direct expropriation is very simple as it takes place by government notification and declaration. Any forceful acquisition, requisition, or forced sale of the property is direct expropriation. In Argentine law, direct expropriation is resorted to when the government, as guarantor of the public interest, needs certain property to satisfy a general and collective community interest and is, therefore, forced to take or use property owned by a person.[6]

6.2.2.2 Indirect Expropriation

As regards indirect expropriation, most of the legal texts include a clause such as "measures having similar effect for expropriation or nationalisation". As mentioned, a similar clause, which refers to indirect expropriation, has been used in section 7 of the FPIA 1980. Exactly which acts or measures constitute indirect expropriation, and the point where different acts or measures reach the stage of being considered an expropriation are not often clearly indicated. Nevertheless, indirect expropriation is explained as an unreasonable government interference with property rights, taking administrative measures, or enacting laws, the practical effect of which would be equivalent to the expropriation, even though the real owner retains the title.[7] In the *Metalclad* award, the tribunal defined it as a "covert or incidental interference with the use of property which has the effect of depriving the owner, in whole or significant part, of the use or reasonably to be expected economic benefit of property even if not necessarily to the obvious benefit of the host state".[8]

An example of a judicial decision creating an expropriation is evident in the International Centre for Settlement of Disputes (ICSID) tribunal's award in *Saipem v Bangladesh.*[9] The *Saipem* ICSID award is probably the first ICSID award to find that the actions of a state court of Bangladesh can have an expropriatory effect. The *Saipem* ICSID tribunal clarified that the actions of Bangladeshi courts in revoking the International Criminal Court (ICC) tribunal's authority and declaring the ICC award a nullity did not constitute a direct expropriation. Instead, such actions constituted 'measures have similar effects' within the meaning of Article 5 (2) of the BIT between the home state of Saipem, Italy and Bangladesh.[10] These actions deprived *Saipem* of the benefit of the ICC award.[11]

The ICSID decision in *Sipem v Bangladesh* declared judicial interference as an indirect expropriation as it caused *Sipem* to lose financial benefits but not control and management over the operation of the company. This decision is contradicted by another ICSID decision in the *CMS Gas Transmission Company v Argentina.*[12] In this case, the tribunal, in setting the criteria for indirect expropriation, denied the existence of an expropriation because the investor had full ownership and control of the investment. The Tribunal considered that expropriation occurs when the investor loses control over the whole investment, thus rejecting the concept of partial expropriation.[13] The decision of the case indicates that partial expropriation by whatever means is not enough to constitute "indirect expropriation".[14]

In the *Saipem v Bangladesh* case, the decision of the ICSID was not based on the substantial loss of Saipem as it acknowledged that "the substantial deprivation of Saipem's ability to enjoy the benefits of the ICC award for compensation from Bangladesh is not sufficient to conclude that Bangladesh courts' intervention is tantamount to an expropriation".[15] This is because the analysis of whether the acts of the judiciary constituted an indirect expropriation was not based on the so-called "sole effects" doctrine. According to this doctrine, the most important aspect of determining indirect investment is the measure's impact; the deprivation has to be substantial to lead to expropriation.[16] Rather, it based its decision on the legality test of Bangladeshi courts' actions to determine whether they amounted to an expropriation. It pointed out that due to the particular circumstances of this dispute and how the parties pleaded their cases, the unlawful character of the actions was a necessary condition.[17]

The point of contention here is that prior awards of ICSID have used only the "sole effect" doctrine, but in the Saipem award, ICSID applied the legality test to determine indirect expropriation. This appears to be a departure from using the "sole effect doctrine" recognised as an important criterion for determining expropriation as established by some other international tribunals where the severity of economic impact is paramount. For example, the European Court of Human Rights has found an expropriation where the investor suffered the substantial deprivation of the enjoyment of ownership and benefit of the property. If the investor's rights have not disappeared but have only been substantially reduced, and the situation is not irreversible, there will be no deprivation under Article 1 of the *European Convention of Human Rights*.[18]

Determining indirect expropriation through a single principle is difficult as it occurs in various circumstances. In its legal effect, there is no distinction between direct and indirect expropriation.[19] The minimum test that can be used for determination is that there is a diminution in the value of the foreign investors' interest in the assets, ownership, control and management of the property, and the period over which it occurs is often longer than necessary. However, this test may be debatable with the increase in governmental intervention in development.

6.2.2.3 Meaning of Public Purpose as a Condition

Regardless of the form, expropriation is legally justified only when two prescribed conditions, public purpose and adequate compensation, are available simultaneously. The national legal texts and BITs uniformly impose a public purpose requirement for expropriation. The word "public purpose" is not defined in the relevant legal text; its extent is not even demarcated by any of the periodic National Industrial Policies (NIPs) in Bangladesh. It generally refers to or is substituted for the word "public interest",[20] which should be determined by the laws and policies of the host state itself. In the *James* case, the Court said that taking property in pursuance of a policy calculated to enhance social justice within the community could properly be described as being "in the public interest".[21] The word "public purpose" may also be explained as taking property for a "social purpose or legal purpose and general welfare that may extend to public health, safety, morals or welfare".[22] Public purpose also covers national economic interest. A noteworthy statement is made by *General Assembly Resolution No. 1803 on Permanent Sovereignty over Natural Resources* under Article 4, which reaffirms the requirement of public purpose, referring to "grounds or reasons of public utility, security or the national interest which are recognized as overriding purely individual or private interest".

Indeed, determining public interests depends upon the host states' internal socio-economic circumstances. Therefore, any undertaking must consider whether it is arbitrary and discriminatory in character or politically motivated.[23]

6.2.2.4 Adequate Compensation as a Condition and Relevant Complicacies

Adequate compensation is another condition for the legal justification of expropriation, whether direct or indirect, legal or illegal. The compensation involved in expropriation is meant to ensure the security of foreign investors' assets and protect their fundamental property rights. It is given in reparation for the loss the investors may have sustained for being deprived of property by expropriation. The economic value of the payment of compensation for host countries is that it safeguards host countries from the negative impact of expropriation and helps them retain the flow of foreign investments.

Determining or calculating the amount of adequate compensation is a major question that is often addressed by the laws of host countries in pursuance of standards set by international law and practices. In Bangladesh, the law refers to the adequate compensation approach in the case of expropriation. Also, it explains the standard of adequate compensation as 'an amount equivalent to the market value of the investment expropriated or nationalized immediately before the expropriation or nationalization'.[24] In addition, regarding the payment method, the law says that the compensation 'shall be paid expeditiously and be freely transferable'.[25] This means that the payment must be made promptly and in easily convertible currency.

The qualification of compensation in these terms in Bangladesh's legal text reveals that the concept of compensation has been borrowed from the traditional Hull formula. Bangladesh has pursued the Hull formula of compensation, which has recently become the subject of much criticism from the host states' economic perspective. The Hull formula holds that compensation must be adequate, effective and prompt. It was dominant during the period of laissez-faire economies and colonisation in the 19th century.[26] The term "adequate" has often been used interchangeably with "full or fair" compensation.[27] This formula represents the concept of full compensation, which, although adopted in different BITs and states' legal texts, has largely failed to provide an agreed-upon normative standard for compensation. It is, therefore, often said to be a long-buried principle.[28]

There are some reasons behind this. The main reason is that the Hull formula was based on Euro-centric values and the notion of the sanctity of private property.[29] It assumed that the character of customary international law was formed with the practice of a few developed capital-exporting states during colonisation and that the vast majority of developing countries had virtually no participation in its formation due to their colonised status. Moreover, today, the traditional consensus, as found in the *Hull formula*, is no longer generally accepted as an expression of customary international law. The consensus has been eroded throughout the 20th century by communist expropriation and nationalisation in many developing countries with the attempt to establish a New International Economic Order through a series of United Nations General Assembly (UNGA) resolutions. The justification is that the formula is not responsive to the needs and goals of developing countries in their work of nation-building. Rather, it is intended to achieve the exclusive profit-maximising objectives of foreign investors in northern countries. Developing countries, therefore, have long been arguing the urgency of modifying the traditional formula of adequate compensation in light of their financial situation and difficulties, which they consider were not of their own making.[30] Developing countries termed this formula an "orthodox standard of compensation", which thwarts their efforts to achieve necessary social and economic reforms. They sought to formulate new laws to govern compensation upon expropriation in consideration of the ability of the expropriating states to pay the amount of compensation.

The expectation of such a governing principle is reflected in Article 2 of the Charter of Economic Rights and Duties 1974, which requires appropriate compensation for nationalisation, expropriation and property transfer. The article suggests that the "appropriate compensation has to be determined by the laws, regulations and other pertinent circumstances of the expropriating states". Furthermore, it allows the settlement of controversy arising over compensation through the mutual agreement of the states based on sovereign equality and the principle of the free choice of means. The developed countries perceive that Article 2 confers upon the host states *carte blanche* powers, allowing them to play the role of judge and jury to their cause in determining compensation.

The term "appropriate compensation" is also affirmed by the World Bank Guidelines.[31] However, this term is clarified differently, as the document establishes a nexus between appropriateness and adequacy of the amount of compensation by saying that "compensation is deemed to be appropriate if it is adequate, effective and prompt". The Guideline attempts to strike a balance between the Hull formula and rules of the Charter as there is no reference to the fact that under cover of "adequate, effective, and prompt", any investor has received full compensation upon the nationalisation or expropriation of their investment.[32] In addition, reviewing some traditional decisions of international tribunals, Professor Schachter remarks that there is no such reference that the decisions of international tribunals have recognised the obligation of adequate, effective and prompt compensation.[33] Given this, applying the Hull formula as an imperative guide for the payment of compensation in the event of nationalisation has become obsolete.

Nevertheless, the Hull formula has still been placed in the national legal texts of foreign investment in many countries, including Bangladesh. It is mostly pursued in the laws and policies of countries that maintain more open and less protective policies to attract foreign investments. Changes and modifications are noticed in the investment legislations of the late 1990s and onwards concerning the standard of the amount of compensation, in the face of the impracticality of the Hull formula on the one hand and the economic and other considerations of the host country on the other hand.[34] The modifications and changes concern replacing the word "adequate" with "appropriate". The word "appropriate" appears to be more logical in that it may provide scope for considering the circumstances that the state considers noteworthy in evaluating the expropriated property to protect the interests of the claimant and its own. An instance is available in the *Aminoil* award where the tribunal considered "appropriate compensation" for a lawful expropriation, although it acknowledged the difficulty in finding the precise meaning of this imprecise term.[35] It observed that

> [...] the determination of the amount of an 'appropriate' compensation is better carried by means of an enquiry into all circumstances relevant to the particular concrete case, than through abstract theoretical discussion.[36]

Whatever the standard of compensation, calculating the value of a nationalised property based on its real or fair market value as established by the majority of national legislations and treaty provisions is a difficult task. However, this market-based approach to valuation is useful when a large number of comparable assets are being traded on financial markets. However, it tends to be more difficult to apply when there are no obvious comparable entities, where little or no revenue is generated, or where it is loss-making.[37] In addition, there may be many considerations and matters to account for in calculating compensation, such as the value of the nationalised assets, the interest gained on the nationalised assets until the awarding of compensation, the issue of the loss of future profits and ongoing concern value.[38] Furthermore, to protect the interests of the host state, the exchange rate and currency valuation at the time of the first investment, the amount of the original investment with the adjustments of re-invested property and the amount of expropriated property should be considered.[39]

6.3 Judicial Arrangement

In Bangladesh, investment-related disputes can be litigated either in the High Court Division (HD) of the Supreme Court or any of three District Judges Courts. The litigation may be lodged with any bench of HD as it has original, appellate, revision and reference jurisdiction.[40] The original jurisdiction of the HD mainly concerns company-related civil matters conferred by *the*

Company Act 1994, the *Admiralty Act 1861* and the *Banking Company Ordinance Act 1962* of Bangladesh.

There is a single company bench formed at the disposal of the Chief Justice that deals with cases related to the management and winding up of the company, the violation of the provisions of the Company Act or Bank-Company Act and investment, trade and other commercial issues. The decision of this court is appealable in the Appellate Division (AD) of the Supreme Court.[41] In the case of writ jurisdiction and the violation of fundamental human rights, the complaint may be lodged with any Bench of the HD of the Supreme Court. The HD is also vested with hearing appeals from District Judge Courts. Any decision of the HD is appealable to the Appellate Division of the Supreme Court.

Apart from the HD, three Judges Courts among the subordinate courts of a civil nature can try investment and trade-related cases. They are the Court of District Judge, the Court of Additional District Judge and the Court of Joint District Judge. These three civil courts have original jurisdictions without any pecuniary limit and appellate jurisdictions. For institution of the proceedings relating to disputes of a civil nature arising out of a breach of contract, breach of trust, land acquisition, breach of property rights, non-payment of compensation for loss or expropriation, repatriation, compensation claims for incidental damages and other business transactions and investments, any party to an investment is entitled to complain about another with any of the District Magistrate Courts.

It is noteworthy that, until now, two cases regarding foreign investment disputes have been lodged with the Court of District Judges in Bangladesh. The first case was lodged against *Saipem S.p.A*, an Italian company that was in contract with Bangladesh in 1990 to install a pipeline. This case was an anti-suit injunction to restrain the ICC tribunal's proceeding. The second case was against Niko Resources Ltd, seeking compensation for environmental damages in *Magur Chara* and *Tengratila.* The proceedings of the trial are still pending.

In addition to such regular courts, there are certain special courts in Bangladesh having specific jurisdiction to decide on commercial and labour disputes constituted under respective laws which have implications for foreign investment. They are (1) Labour Courts; (2) Income Tax Appellate Tribunals; (3) *Artha Rin Adalats* (Money Loan Court); and (4) Insolvency Courts. The Labour Courts as established under the *BLA 2006* deal with labour disputes as defined by the *Act.*[42] The Income Tax Appellate Tribunals decide income tax disputes and customs and excise matters.[43] The *Artha Rin Adalats* decide money claims of banks and other financial institutions.[44] The Insolvency Courts declare defaulting borrowers as insolvent.[45]

The judicial arrangements for settling investment disputes appear reasonably adequate in Bangladesh, although there is no special economic court for dealing with foreign investment-related disputes as in China. In particular, the designated Bench in the apex constitutional court testifies that company and investment issues are highly regarded. However, because there is a single Bench, it is often overburdened with cases.

6.4 Internal Arbitral Arrangement

Alongside the judicial arrangement, arbitration is increasingly being employed as a method of investment-related dispute settlement in Bangladesh, and it has proved to be a successful and efficient means of conflict resolution of commercial matters. Although the foreign investors are not in general so far interested in invoking internal arbitration arrangements for settling disputes with host state parties, some joint-venture investment agreements, for example, the agreement between Niko Resources and Bangladesh,[46] have opted for internal arbitration as an alternative to courts, particularly after developing an internal arbitration system by enacting the *Arbitration Act 2001* (hereinafter referred to as the *Act of 2001*).[47] In addition, some arbitral institutions are developed at the local level to settle disputes.

The *Act of 2001* is the fundamental instrument for regulating all commercial arbitrations in Bangladesh. It establishes the legal framework for international commercial arbitration and the recognition and enforcement of foreign arbitral awards and domestic arbitration in Bangladesh.[48] The term "international commercial arbitration", as defined in section 2(c) of this Act, covers commercial disputes arising from a legal relationship involving a foreign investment agreement.[49] This new law was amended in 2004 in certain respects, and some supplementary legislative provisions were introduced in response to increasing foreign investment in Bangladesh in various sectors, prominently natural gas and power and the emerging international export trade.

One of the fundamental features of the *Act of 2001* is that it is principally based on the *UNCITRAL Model Law on International Commercial Arbitration.*[50] However, it does not contain the same law as the model law, as it borrowed some provisions from the *Indian Arbitration and Conciliation Act 1996*.[51] The Act follows the same provisions of the model law in the definition and formation of an arbitration agreement, the composition of an arbitral tribunal, the insertion of an arbitration clause in the contract, the setting aside of an arbitral award and so on.[52] Thus, it creates a distinctive and unified legal regime for arbitration that is an alternative to judicial settlement. The uniqueness of this Act also lies in its comprehensive feature that covers parties' all procedural rights to justice in pre-award and post-award stages of arbitration, including the enforcement mechanism of the award decided under this law and the enforcement of foreign arbitral awards at the local level.

To offer or ensure a fair and just arbitral system for international commercial dispute resolution, the *Act of 2001* pursues international standards in procedural issues such as the composition of arbitral tribunals, the appointment of an arbitrator,[53] the jurisdiction of the tribunals,[54] the conduct of proceedings,[55] the making of arbitral awards,[56] the right of recourse against arbitral awards,[57] and the fundamental tenets of modernisation of international arbitration, mainly focused on (i) party autonomy; (ii) minimal judicial intervention in arbitration; (iii) independence of the arbitral tribunal; (iv) fair, expeditious and economical resolution of disputes; and (v) the effective enforcement of arbitral awards.[58] Apart from this, the *Act of 2001*, for the first time in Bangladesh's arbitral history, has set out a comprehensive enforcement mechanism for domestic or foreign arbitral awards involving the existing judiciary.

To appreciate the features, firstly about party autonomy, the contracting parties enjoy enormous autonomy mainly on two grounds: participation in the arbitration process and the application of governing laws to be used for the settlement of disputes if they wish to seek arbitration under this Act as a means of conflict resolution. According to this Act, the parties can invoke arbitration under the Act only when they have mutually inserted an "arbitration clause" in their business agreements to settle any dispute arising out of the breach of the agreement.[59] The Act has pursued corresponding international development and introduced the clause "autonomy of arbitration" in the context of the jurisdiction of arbitral awards.

Secondly, as regards the independence of the arbitral tribunal, according to this Act, the arbitral tribunal is formed independently of judicial intervention. The judiciary has no power to deal with the appointment of arbitration except in the case of urgency. The composition of the arbitral tribunal and the number of arbitrators indeed depend upon the rules chosen by the parties.[60] Subject to some restrictions, the parties can enjoy freedom under the new Act to agree on a procedure for appointing an arbitrator or arbitrators.[61] In response to the recent trend towards the internationalisation of arbitration, the new law does not restrict the nationality of arbitrators. It leaves the matter to the parties' choice.[62]

As regards the tribunal's independence, it is noteworthy that, as mentioned earlier, it is only bound by the laws the parties agree to apply to conduct arbitration. Therefore, it is not bound to comply with the provisions of the *Code of Civil Procedures 1908* and the *Evidence Act 1872* in disposing of a dispute under the Act. Even an arbitral award need not state any reason for parties not to be given.

Thirdly, as far as judicial intervention is concerned, the new law strives to create an impartial arbitration climate in Bangladesh, where judicial intervention is meagre and negligent. There are certain rare situations when the judiciary can participate in arbitration activities to a limited extent.[63]

Fourthly, the prime objective of the Act is to ensure fair, expeditious and economical resolution of disputes. To attain this objective, the Act introduces a competitive procedural framework of arbitration that ensures access to justice for an aggrieved party. To ensure procedural fairness and impartiality for arbitral decision-making, the *Act* endorses certain principles of natural justice as imperatives for arbitral tribunals in conducting their proceedings. These include (i) giving each party a reasonable opportunity to present its case orally, in writing, or both and (ii) giving each party a reasonable opportunity to examine all the documents and other relevant materials furnished by the other party or any other person concerned before the tribunal.[64] In addition to procedural fairness, the *Act* provides a swift procedural arrangement for seeking remedy by arbitration and, therefore, prescribes the place and location of arbitration in Bangladesh so that all of the resolution activities can be accomplished within a reasonably short time and with less expense.

Concerning the effective enforcement of domestic or foreign arbitral awards, the Act adopts some ways, the most important of which is that it has accorded every arbitral award the status of a decree of a civil court, thus making the institutional participation of judicial administration essential, for the enforcement of a decree of its own. It, therefore, says that the award shall be enforced under the *Code of Civil Procedure* (CPC) of Bangladesh in the same manner as if it were a decree of the Court.[65] This means that on the application being made to it by any party, the Court under the CPC will execute the award in the prescribed way as required for its decree. Another important feature is that the Act, for the first time, has incorporated the mechanism of the *New York Convention* to recognise and enforce foreign arbitral awards in Chapter X.[66] This chapter exclusively deals with foreign awards under the title "Recognition and Enforcement of Certain Foreign Arbitral Awards". It focuses on a general principle that "any foreign award which will be enforceable shall be treated as binding for all purposes on the persons as between whom it was made, any award may accordingly be relied upon by any of those persons by way of defense, set off or otherwise in any legal proceedings in Bangladesh".[67] The HD is empowered to oversee the enforcement of foreign arbitral awards. However, the Act also provides the grounds for the refusal of the award, including *inter alia* legal incapacities and the question of the validity of an arbitration agreement between the parties, the absence of proper notification for the presentation of a case, the lack of arbitral scope for the case and the violation of an agreement in the appointment of arbitrators.[68]

Given the aforesaid discussion, the relevant provisions under the *Act of 2001* regarding the arbitration of a commercial dispute arising out of local and international business or investment seem to be comprehensive, neutral, modern and internationalised. They also seem capable of protecting the parties' interests by ensuring justice. As argued, the arbitration environment in Bangladesh has changed substantially following the introduction of the Act, and it appears now to be more "arbitration-friendly".[69] Accordingly, there is a general rise in arbitration as an alternate dispute resolution. Disputes arising from construction, engineering and infrastructure contracts are often called arbitration.[70]

6.5 Application of International Arbitration

Bangladesh recognises the jurisdictions of internationally recognised arbitral bodies such as the ICC Court of Arbitration and the ICSID through mutual negotiations under BITs. Apart from BITs, Bangladesh also accepts its jurisdiction under specific contracts such as Joint Venture Contracts (JVAs), Product Sharing Contracts (PSCs), Gas Purchase and Sale Agreements (GPSAs) and International Purchase Agreements.

As regards reference to the ICC, some recent BITs, including Bangladesh's Model BIT, provide for resorting to ICC jurisdiction in disputes relating to the interpretation and the application provisions of the agreements. However, in the past, the ICC court was used to settle disputes between foreign investors and Bangladesh. For example, Bangladesh signed a BIT with Italy in 1992, and according to this, Saipem, an Italian entity, and Bangladesh Oil Gas and Mineral Corporation (Petrobangla) entered into a pipeline construction contract to be governed by the laws of Bangladesh. It provided for disputes to be resolved by arbitration under the ICC Rules to be held in Dhaka. The following is the arbitration clause:

> If any dispute, question or difference should arise between the parties to this contract with regard to rights and obligations hereunder which cannot be settled amicably, such dispute, question or difference shall be finally settled under the Rules of Conciliation and Arbitration of the International Chamber of Commerce by three arbitrators.... The venue of the arbitration shall be Dhaka. The Procedure in arbitration shall be in English.[71]

Although the ICC arbitration is seen to have been chosen under a specific investment contract, the present trend is that the arbitration is mostly sought by the ICSID.

ICSID is another institution of international arbitration with jurisdiction Bangladesh accepts by its accession into the establishing Convention, as indicated earlier. It was established under the auspices of the World Bank. ICSID came into being by the Convention on the Settlement of Investment Disputes between States and Nationals of other States,[72] which came into force on 14 October 1976. Bangladesh became a party to it in 1980. Since then, the ICSID arbitration jurisdiction has been consistently and prominently pursued in BITs, along with others, as one method of settlement in disputes concerning investments between Bangladesh and investors of other contracting countries.

Bangladesh has so far concluded BITs with 36 countries, and except for a few, such as the BIT between Bangladesh and Germany, they all reference ICSID arbitration for dispute settlements as an alternative to a domestic court. In particular, the *Model Agreement 2009*, for the promotion and protection of foreign investment, provides a guideline for settling investment-related disputes where international arbitration through ICSID is emphasised as an option. Article 13 of the *Model Agreement* suggests as follows:

> The international arbitration may be held by the International Centre for Settlement of Investment Disputes for settlement by arbitration under Washington Convention, 1965 provided that both the parties are parties to the Convention. The arbitration award under ICSID shall be binding on both the parties and shall not be subject to any appeal or remedy other than those provided in the said convention.

In addition, the ICSID provision for the enforcement of an arbitral award by the domestic court in accordance with domestic law has also been confirmed by the provision of the Model Agreement. The *Arbitration Act of 2001* also articulates a procedure for enforcing a foreign arbitral award.[73]

Given the above discussion, it is clear that in the absence of any explicit reference in national FDI legislation or policies, in Bangladesh, the guidance for dispute settlement mechanisms has been settled through bilateral treaty negotiations, and in that respect, international arbitration as a neutral platform between investors and the host state has been well recognised. Moreover, being party to the ICSID and ICC, Bangladesh shows its commitment to permitting investors to exercise their right to access justice, and thus, their legal protection is guaranteed. It is noteworthy that Bangladesh has so far participated in three ICSID arbitral cases known as the Niko, Saipem and Chevron cases.[74]

6.6 The Conflicting Situations between Foreign Investors and Bangladesh

6.6.1 Foreign Investors' Negative Attitude towards National Courts

In recent times, some studies and reports on the existing investment climate in Bangladesh have revealed investors' negative attitudes towards the judicial protection available in Bangladesh for dispute resolution.[75] They point out some operational weaknesses and inabilities of the enforcement mechanism of the existing judiciary, including the disqualification of judges to deal with international commercial issues. They also argue the existence of weak and cumbersome judicial procedures, wide corruption in the judiciary (particularly in the lower courts), delays in tort judgments due to the absence of a prescribed penalty provision, judges' ignorance of international accounting practices, procedural weaknesses and delays in the enforcement of awards and a scarcity of competent judges both in lower and upper courts.[76]

The tendency of avoidance in some cases is promoted either by the scope of simultaneous use of a domestic court and international arbitration or the scope of direct resort to international arbitration under an investment agreement between Bangladesh and a foreign company. The recent Niko case evidences this. In this case, when Bangladesh part filed a lawsuit against *Niko* for damages out of the *Tengratila* blowout in 2008, *Niko* prepared to defend the lawsuit. During the continuation of the proceedings of the suit, *Niko* proceeded to ICSID with an arbitration suit to settle the case over the compensation issue and to realise their outstanding gas bill for the gas field project.[77] *Niko* did this by applying the "arbitration clause" for dispute settlement under the joint venture agreement between Niko and Bangladesh Petroleum and Production Company.[78]

The tendency to avoid using domestic courts in favour of international arbitration based on common complaints can result in disregarding national laws. When investment disputes are commonly taken to international arbitration, bypassing domestic judicial resolution, it raises the issue of whether local remedies can be bypassed by mutual agreement. This question will be addressed in a separate section. However, this practice has a downside: it may impede legal development and the rule of law in Bangladesh's foreign investment sector. Foreign investors' persistent reluctance to engage with national courts due to genuine concerns about infrastructural inefficiencies or quality issues will hinder the judiciary's future development in this area.

6.6.2 Foreign Investors' Negative Attitude towards the Internal Arbitral System

Foreign investors hold a similar attitude towards internal arbitration to local courts; they are not interested in internal arbitration for dispute settlement. The state parties under BITs or individual investors' contracts with Bangladesh are seldom seen to invoke internal arbitration for the settlement of disputes. Despite the newly introduced arbitration system being modern and internationalised, the reason for their reservations is revealed particularly by the experiences of the *Saipem* and *Chevron* cases.[79] This includes two aspects of the Act of 2001: first, that Dhaka is the prescribed location of arbitration under this Act, as opposed to the customary practice of arbitration being held in a neutral country, and second, that the Act is more specific to Bangladesh.[80]

The first point is that Dhaka is not a neutral place for arbitration, which may be acceptable because its location goes against customary practice. However, location is not the only factor in creating a neutral approach. For example, regional arbitration centres, such as those under the ICC Court of Arbitration, play an important role, and Dhaka is one of these. Additionally, the ICSID arbitration centre is located in Washington, where arbitration matters placed by US companies are entertained. The second reason for reluctance to utilise

Bangladesh's arbitration system is baseless, as the arbitration jurisdiction under the Act extends to settling disputes relating to international commercial transactions between Bangladesh and others. This is a common feature of all national arbitration legislation dealing with foreign cases. Therefore, protesting that the Act is specific to Bangladesh is not rational. It is also noteworthy that the law allows the other party to select arbitrators, including foreign nationals, to maintain impartiality in arbitral proceedings. The local court has no scope of interference in this process unless a conflict arises in selecting arbitrators or parties fail to select an arbitrator.[81]

Apart from the above two reservation points, enforcing arbitral awards is also a grave concern of foreign investors as it suffers numerous institutional, legal, infrastructural, cultural and educational problems. Their grounds of reservation are also corroborated by a study that has identified the following factors barring the arbitral awards[82]:

1 The local courts, as an enforcing machinery, have some anti-arbitration bias and a tendency towards non-cooperation.
2 The local courts lack the aptitude to appreciate the mores and ethos of international private dispute settlement.
3 There is a serious lack of understanding of international rules and conventions including the *New York Convention.*
4 The courts have local protectionism.
5 There is widespread corruption among various levels of administration and the judiciary.
6 The system is sometimes manipulated by local disputing parties.

The above factors are not only the case with the courts of Bangladesh but are a common phenomenon in third-world countries where the courts suffer multiple types of legal infrastructural inefficiency, and corruption is paramount. However, local protectionism is not unjustified if it becomes an essential consideration under special circumstances. According to the Act, the court can avoid enforcement if the matter proves incapable of arbitration or if the award enforcement opposes Bangladesh's public policy.[83] This protective provision appears to be very logical in terms of the interest of the host country. It cannot be denied that the judiciary in Bangladesh has multiple logistical incapacities and is also infected with corruption and potential manipulation. Still, in the case of enforcing foreign arbitral awards (which involve the country's economic interests), the author believes that the government will try its utmost to retain a positive image of the country. Moreover, the *Act of 2001* empowered the HD to oversee enforcement, which is less corrupt than the lower courts. Nevertheless, the government should address these issues to earn the confidence of the international business community and simultaneously establish a strong internal arbitral system.

6.6.3 The Negative Attitudes of the Government of Bangladesh to International Arbitration

Bangladesh has participated in several international arbitration proceedings with foreign investors under the ICC and ICSID arbitral regimes. In different arbitration proceedings, the counterpart foreign investors are Chevron, *Saipem S.P.A, Niko* and Lahmeyer International Polly Power Services.[84] The experiences of all these international arbitration proceedings have shown a different picture and raised considerable doubts about the government of Bangladesh's inclination to voluntary compliance with arbitration proceedings. However, the government also has some grounds for allegations against the neutrality of international arbitration.

In this respect, an empirical study argues that whenever a dispute is brought to international arbitration, despite a seemingly strong commitment on paper, the government is found to be reluctant, as if the original agreement has been forgotten.[85] It is quite often that faced with claims of a breach of its contractual or investment obligation in international arbitrations, the government either vehemently denies participating in the original dispute settlement proceedings or applies some tactics to frustrate the arbitration proceedings by raising issues that appear to be unjustifiable and unsound in law. Sometimes, during arbitral proceedings for dispute resolution, the government manifestly exploits its judicial system and local laws to gain the advantage of anti-suit injunctions or to evade international awards rendered against it. This is evident in *Saipem S.p.A v Bangladesh*, where the government of Bangladesh (Petrobangla), after a ruling by ICC in favour of Saipem for damages, moved first to the local District Judge Court seeking an anti-suit injunction and then to the HD. The HD issued an injunction declaring that the ICC arbitral proceeding was illegal and without jurisdiction.

The study also finds that the government's reluctance to participate in international arbitrations mainly manifests in its effort to avoid the jurisdiction of international arbitration. To avoid jurisdiction, the government pleads on some common grounds, such as that the dispute falls outside the scope of the arbitration agreement, or the government is not a party to the contract, and the arbitration obligation under a BIT does not apply.[86] In the arbitration case under ICSID between Chevron and Bangladesh, the government of Bangladesh objected to the jurisdiction of ICSID. The dispute was related to the non-payment of four percent of sale proceeds by *Petrobangla* (a public entity in Bangladesh), which was first endeavoured to be resolved amicably. Failing this, Chevron lodged the case with ICSID for arbitration, making Bangladesh a defendant with *Petrobangla*. Bangladesh contested ICSID's jurisdiction on two grounds. Firstly, the dispute in question "is not even [an] investment dispute" according to its ordinary meaning as the meaning of investing refers, according to the government, to the "investing of money" to earn interest and bring profit.[87] Therefore, neither the "exploration, development, and other operations" nor "the sale of gas" constitutes investments under Article 25 (1) of the *ICSID Convention*. Secondly, it was argued that the dispute is not between a Contracting state and a national of another Contracting State, as Petrobangla is not part of the government. On the other hand, Chevron is a national of Bermuda, which is not a party to ICSID. ICSID denied these contentions. It found that the meaning of investment does not conflict with Article 25 (1) of the Convention and that the contractual dispute arose directly from the investment. In determining the second question about the government of Bangladesh's responsibility for *Petrobangla*, the tribunal found that *Petrobangla* is a *de jure* organ of the government whose actions are attributable to it.[88]

The government has reasons for not adhering to international arbitration commitments. Officials sometimes justify this by citing reasons such as lack of cultural awareness, inadequate legal skills for international arbitration, bias from arbitrators and disregard for environmental regulation and human rights protection by the tribunal.[89] The government's such reluctance to adhere to international arbitration tribunals, whether justified or not, could jeopardise Bangladesh's standing in international contracts and treaties. This may lead to losing the trust of other countries and harm Bangladesh's reputation as an investment-friendly nation. The Chevron saga is a prime example of this, as the UK embassy officials have expressed concern about the government's repeated involvement in the dispute, which has harmed foreign investors.[90]

6.7 Concluding Remarks

It is crucial to ensure that the measures for protecting national interests do not undermine the advantages that FDI can bring to a country. Therefore, it is crucial to establish the appropriate rules and systems to protect the interests of all parties involved in FDI. A well-structured dispute resolution system, supported by a strong commitment to implementing its decisions, should be at the core of this framework.

The current dispute resolution system between foreign investors and the government in Bangladesh has resulted in a lack of trust. To address this issue, this country needs to incorporate specific provisions in national legislation, bilateral investment treaties and individual agreements between the involved parties. The regulatory provisions should particularly focus on the following matters:

- Introduce a specific core principle for resolving disputes in our national FDI legislation, along with a clear definition of jurisdiction and a dispute resolution clause based on mutual agreement.

- Mandate the use of local remedies in FDI legislation and ensure compliance with the requirements in BITs between the contracting state parties.
- Permit the transfer of dispute resolution to international arbitration through mutual consent, with limitations on unilateral transfers during local court proceedings.
- Set a timeframe for local civil courts to enforce arbitral awards and designate the High Court Division of the Supreme Court of Bangladesh to take responsibility if this is not carried out.
- Specify the access to international arbitration in BITs or individual investment agreements.
- Expand the scope of dispute resolution to include labour, environment and human rights issues by mutual consent between investors and Bangladesh.
- Propose the establishment of a region-based arbitral centre by ICSID to bridge cultural gaps and reduce associated costs for countries in South and East Asia.

Notes

1 See the Agreement Between the Government of the Philippines and the Government of People's Republic of Bangladesh for the Promotion and Reciprocal Protection of Investments (1998), the Agreement Between the Government of the Republic of Indonesia and the Government of the Republic of India for the Promotion and Protection of Investments (2004), Agreement Between the Republic of Austria and the People's Republic of Bangladesh for the Promotion and Protection of Investments (2001), Agreement Between the Government of Canada and the Government of the Kingdom of Thailand (1998), Agreement Between the People's Republic of Bangladesh and the Swiss Confederation on the Promotion and Reciprocal Protection of Investments. For more about this, visit UNCTAD, Investment Instruments Online <http://www.unctadix.org/templates/page_1007.aspx> 20 May 2024.

2 *The National Industrial Policy (Bangladesh)* 2010, Ch. 13.

3 *The Constitution of the Republic of Croatia* (2010) art. 5, para 1.

4 See, for example, in the BIT between Bangladesh and Thailand, article 5(b) of the treaty stated that the legality of any expropriation and the amount and method of payment of compensation shall be subject to review by due process of law. Article 5(1) of the BIT between Bangladesh and the United Arab Emirates, it is mentioned that "investment shall not be nationalized … except for expropriation made in the public interest, on a basis of non-discrimination, carried out under due process of, and against prompt, adequate and effective compensation."

5 M Sornarajah, *The International Law on Foreign Investment* (Cambridge, 3rd ed., 2010) 364.

6 Wenhua Shah (ed.), *The Legal Protection of Foreign Investment: A Comparative Study* (Hart Publishing, 2012) 111.

7 See Starret Housing Corp. et al. and the Government of the Islamic Republic of Iran et al. (United States Claims Tribunals, Rep.122–154, 1983). This case dealt with the appointment of Iranian Managers to an American housing project. The Tribunal concluded that an expropriation had taken place.

8 *Metalclad v. Mexico* (2000) 5 ICSID Reports, page 209, para 103.

9 See *Saipem S.p.A. v. The People's Republic of Bangladesh* (2009) ICSID Case No. ARB/05/7, unreported, para 124.

10 Article 5(2) states that investments of investors of one of the Contracting Parties shall not be directly or indirectly nationalised, expropriated, requisitioned, or subjected to any measures having similar effects in the territory of the other Contracting party, except for public purposes, or national interest, against immediate, full, and effective compensation, and on condition that these measures are taken on a non-discriminatory basis or in conformity with all legal provisions and procedures. (Agreement of 20 March 1990 between the Government of the Republic of Italy and the Government of the People's Republic of Bangladesh on the Promotion and Protection of Investment. The treaty entered into force on 20 September 1994.)

11 *Saipem v. Bangladesh,* above n 9, 129.

12 (2003) ICSID Case No. ARB/01/8, paras 263–64.

13 U Kriebaum, 'Partial Expropriation' (2007) 8 (1) *The Journal of World Investment and Trade* 69, 74.

14 In Tipples v TAMS –ATTA, it was observed that "constructive expropriation" occurs when events demonstrate that the owner was deprived of fundamental rights of ownership and that this deprivation is not merely ephemeral. See *Tipples v TAMS-ATTA* (1985) 6 Iran-US CTR 219–225.

15 *Saipem v Bangladesh,* above n 9, 133.

16 *Saipem v Bangladesh,* above n 9, 133.

17 *Saipem v Bangladesh,* above n 9, 134.

18 See cases *Handyside* v *United Kingdom (*1976) 24 Eur.Ct.H.R. (ser.A) 29; *Poiss v Austria* (1987) 117 Eur.Ct.H.R.(ser.A) 84,108. See discussion H. Ruiz Fabri, 'The Approach Taken by the European Court of Human Rights to the Assessment of Compensation for "Regulatory Appropriations of the Property of Foreign Investors"' (2002) 2(1) *N.Y.U Environmental Law Journal* 148, 152.

19 See *Biloune v Ghana Investment Board* (1993) 95 ILR 184, para 75. The tribunal held that no distinction should be drawn between direct and creeping expropriation.

20 Andrew Newcombe and Lluis Paradell, *Law and Practice of Investment Treaties: Standards of Treatment* (Kluwer Law International, 2009) 370.

21 This case concerns a reform undertaken by the United Kingdom regarding the right of individuals with long leases to acquire the freehold of their leasehold property. This reform, according to James, the Claimant, "deprived" the freeholders of their property since they could neither refuse to sell nor set the price for it. See *James v United Kingdom* (1986) 98 Eur. Ct. H.R. (ser.A) 9, 32.

22 G Christie, 'What Constitutes a Taking of Property under International Law?' (1962) 38 *British Yearbook of International Law* 307, 338.

23 *Lybian American Oil Company Limco v. Lybia* (1981) 20 ILM 1 288, 408, 430, 431.

24 *Foreign Private (Promotion and Protection) Investment Act* (Bangladesh) 1980 s. 7(2) (1).

25 *Foreign Private (Promotion and Protection) Investment Act* (Bangladesh) 1980 s. 7(2) (1).

26 In 1938, the United States Secretary of State Hull, in response to the Mexican agrarian nationalisation measures, declared in correspondence to the Ambassador of Mexico that under every rule of law and equity, no government is entitled to expropriate private property, for whatever purpose, without provision for prompt, adequate and effective payment thereof. Since that time, this phrase (prompt, adequate and effective) has sometimes been referred to as the "Hull Formula". See Louis Henkin et al., *International Law: Cases and Materials* (West Publication Co., 1980) 688.

27 According to Schwarzenberger, the difference between "full" and "adequate" compensation is merely one between synonyms; see G Schwarzenberger, *Foreign Investment and International Law* (London, 1969) 10.

28 M Rafiqul Islam, *International Trade Law* (Law Book Company, Australia, 1999) 246.
29 M Rafiqul Islam, *International Trade Law* (Law Book Company, Australia, 1999) 246.
30 Sherif H Seid, *Global Regulation of Foreign Direct Investment* (Ashgate Publishing Company, 2002) 47.
31 See *World Bank Guidelines on the Treatment of Foreign Direct Investment* (1992), art. IV.
32 For examples, major 20th-century deprivation settlements, notably Mexican agrarian policies, Eastern European nationalisation programmes, the taking of the oil industry in the wake of a change of government in Libya and the Iranian concessionary contracts, show that the claimant states have never received "adequate, effective and prompt" compensation. In all cases, less than full compensation has been paid to the owners of the alien property and in instalments. See M Bulajic, *Principles of International Development Law* (Marinus Nijhoff, 1993) 264; Dawson and B Weston, 'Prompt, Adequate and Effective: A Universal Standard of Compensation' (1961–1962) 30 (4) *Fordham Law Review* 727, 728; Islam, above n 29, 251.
33 O Schachter, 'Compensation for Expropriation' (1984) 78 (1) *American Journal of International Law* 122, 123.
34 O Schachter, 'Compensation for Expropriation' (1984) 78 (1) *American Journal of International Law* 122, 123.
35 *Kuwait v American Independent Oil Company* (1982) 21 ILM, 976, 1032.
36 *Kuwait v American Independent Oil Company* (1982), para. 144.
37 A Damodran, *Investment Valuation* (John Wiley and Sons, London, 2002) 1.4. Damodran notes that often uncertainty comes from the asset being valued, though the valuation model may add to that uncertainty. See also Sergey Ripinsky and Kevin Williams, *Damages in International Investment Law* (British Institute of International and Comparative Law, 2008) 214.
38 See Islam, above n 29, 251.
39 See Islam, above n 29, 251.
40 See *the Constitution of People's Republic of Bangladesh* (1972) arts. 103, 101 and 102 (2). Article 101 states that the High Court Division shall have such original, appellate and other jurisdictions, powers and functions as are or may be conferred on it by this Constitution on any other.
41 The Appellate Division of the Supreme Court is the highest court with jurisdiction over appeals, issuance and execution of process and advisory review.
42 See *the Bangladesh Labour Act 2006* (Bangladesh) ss. 214–218.
43 See *the Income Tax Ordinance 1984* (Bangladesh) ss. 11–15.
44 See *the Artho Rin Adalat Act 2003* (Bangladesh) s. 5.
45 See *the Bankruptcy Act 1997* (Bangladesh) s. 5.
46 *Joint Venture Agreement for the Development and Production of Petroleum from the Marginal /Abandoned Chattok and Feni Gas Field Niko Resource (Bangladesh) Limited and Bangladesh Petroleum Exploration and Production Company Limited* (2003) art. 18(3) and 18(4).
47 This Act came into force on 10 April 2001 by repealing the previous Arbitration (Protocol and Convention) Act 1937 and the Arbitration 1940.
48 See the preamble of the *Arbitration Act 2001* as worded, "An Act to enact the law relating to international commercial arbitration, recognition and enforcement of foreign arbitral awards and other arbitrations".
49 Section 2 (c) states that international commercial arbitration means an arbitration relating to disputes arising out of legal "relationships, whether contractual or not, considered as commercial under the law in force in Bangladesh and where at least one of the parties is - (i) an individual who is a national of or habitually resident

in, any country other than Bangladesh; (ii) a body corporate which is incorporated in any country other Bangladesh; (iii) a company or an association or a body of individuals whose central management and control is exercised in any country other than Bangladesh."

50 *UNCITRAL Model Law on International Commercial Arbitration* (U.N. GAOR, 40th Sess., Annex I, U.N. Doc. A/40/17, Annex 1, 1985) <http://www.uncitral.org/en-index.htm> 25 May 2024.

51 See AFM Maniruzzaman, 'The New Law of International Commercial Arbitration in Bangladesh: A Comparative Perspective' (2003) 14 *American Review of International* Arbitration 139, 142–171.

52 See *UNICITRAL Model Law*, Articles 8, 10, 16, 34.

53 See *the Arbitration Act 2001* (Bangladesh) s. 12.

54 See *the Arbitration Act 2001* (Bangladesh) s. 17.

55 See *the Arbitration Act 2001* (Bangladesh) ss. 23–35.

56 See *the Arbitration Act 2001* (Bangladesh) ss. 36–41

57 See *the Arbitration Act 2001* (Bangladesh) ss. 42–44.

58 Maniruzzaman, above n 53, 171.

59 *The Arbitration Act 2001* (Bangladesh), s. 4(2).

60 *The Arbitration Act 2001* (Bangladesh), s. 11 (1).

61 *The Arbitration Act 2001* (Bangladesh), s. 12(1).

62 *The Arbitration Act 2001* (Bangladesh), s. 12(2).

63 Firstly, under the default procedure of this law, as mentioned earlier, the Chief Justice of the Supreme Court is allowed to deal with the appointment of arbitrators. Secondly, the Chief Justice is vested with the power to supervise international commercial arbitration within the scope allowed by the Act. Thirdly, the High Court Division has the power to decide on the matter of jurisdiction if it is satisfied that the determination of the question is likely to produce substantial savings in cost, the application is submitted without any delay, and there is a good reason as to why the matter should be decided by the court. It is thus clear that the High Court Division cannot decide such jurisdictional questions of its own volition. Fourthly, pursuant to Section 10 (2), the Court, if it is satisfied that an arbitration agreement exists, refers the parties to the arbitration and stays the proceedings (if the action brought before it) unless it finds that the arbitration agreement is void, inoperative, or incapable of determination by arbitration. Fifthly, the judicial authority can interfere with arbitration only on public policy grounds.

64 *The Arbitration Act 2001* (Bangladesh) s. 23(1) (a), (b).

65 *The Arbitration Act 2001* (Bangladesh), ss. 44 and 45 (1) (b).

66 It is noted that before the enactment of the present legislation on arbitration in 2001, there existed no legal mechanism for enforcing a foreign arbitral award in Bangladesh. Although Bangladesh acceded to the *New York Convention* on 6 July 1992, it has not yet enacted any enabling statute to give effect to the Convention itself. Hence, the Bangladesh Courts are very reluctant to apply the New York Convention to the issue of recognition and enforcement of foreign arbitral awards.

67 *The Arbitration Act 2001* (Bangladesh) s. 45 (a).

68 See *The Arbitration Act 2001* (Bangladesh) s. 46. It notes that the award may be refused on the grounds that (1) a party to the arbitration agreement had some legal incapacities; (2) that the arbitration agreement was not valid under the law to which the parties are subjected; or (3) that the party against whom the award is given was not given proper notice appointment of the arbitrator or of the arbitral proceedings and accordingly was unable to present his case; or (4) that the decisions of the arbitral awards are beyond the scope of arbitral reference; or (5) that the composition of arbitration tribunal was in violation the arbitration agreement or the state law of the place of the arbitration; or (6) that the award was set aside or suspended by

the competent authority of the country, or under the law of which, that award was made; or (6) that the dispute was not fit for settlement by arbitration under the law or was to opposed to public policy.

69 See Ajmalul Hossain QC, 'Bangladesh' in Andreas Respondek (ed.), *Asia Arbitration Guide* (Respondek and Fan Pte Ltd, 2011) 23 <https://www.rf-arbitration.com> 1 June 2024.

70 Thomas J. Stipanowich, T. J. (2010). Arbitration: The new litigation. 1 *University of Illinois Law Review*, 1–61.

71 Thomas J. Stipanowich, T. J. (2010). Arbitration: The new litigation. 1 *University of Illinois Law Review*, 1–61.

72 See, the decision on jurisdiction and recommendation on provisional measures provided in *Saipem S.p.A v Bangladesh* IIC 280 (2007).

73 It is popularly called the *Washington Convention*. Here in the *Convention*, "Nationals of other States" means the nationals of another Contracting State, including both natural and juridical persons (see Article 25 of the *Convention*). ICSID gives private investors direct access to an international forum. The jurisdiction of ICSID is limited in that one of the parties must be a contracting state, and the other must be a national of another contracting state. However, ICSID will administer proceedings that fall outside the scope of the convention.

74 *The Arbitration Act 2001* (Bangladesh), ss. 45 (a), 46.

75 Saipem v Bangladesh dealt with the pecuniary jurisdiction of USD 12.6 million (see *Saipem S.p.A v the People's Republic of Bangladesh* (2009) ICSID Case No. ARB/05/07), Chevron v Bangladesh dealt with the pecuniary jurisdiction of USD 127 million (see *Chevron Bangladesh Block Twelve Ltd and Chevron Bangladesh Blocks Thirteen and Fourteen Ltd v People's Republic of Bangladesh* (2010) ICSID Case No. ARB/06/10), Niko v Bangladesh dealt with the pecuniary jurisdiction of USD 35.71 million (see *Niko Resources Bangladesh Ltd v Bangladesh Petroleum Exploration and Production Company Ltd and Bangladeshi Oil, Gas and Mineral Corporation* (2013) ICSID Case No. ARB/08/10).

76 See US Department of Justice, *Investment Climate in Bangladesh* ((2010) <http://www.state.gov/e/eb/rls/othr/ ics/2012/191106.htmBangladesh> 1June 2024; see also the World Bank and Bangladesh Enterprise Institute, *Improving the Investment Climate in* (June 2003) <www.bdresearch.org.bd/home/ attachments/ article/486/ Bdesh_ICA-Proof_2pdf> 1 June 2024.

77 M I Faruque, Sajed A Sami and Taslima Yasmin, 'Impact of International Arbitration Proceeding: Governmental Approach and Investment Climate in Bangladesh' (Working Paper No. 1, Economic Research Group, Bangladesh, June 2010) <http://www.ergonline.org/ifc/index_of_SGAPP.html> 1st June 2024.

78 See *Niko Resources Bangladesh Ltd v Bangladesh Petroleum Exploration and Production Company Limited and Bangladesh Oil, Gas and Mineral Corporation* (2013) ICSID Cases No. ARB/10/11 and ARB8/10.

79 See *Joint Venture Agreement for the Development and Production of Petroleum from the Marginal/Abandoned Chattok and FenI Gas Field* between Niko Resources (Bangladesh) Limited and Bangladesh (2003) art. 18.

80 Faruque, Sami and Yasmin, above n 77.

81 Faruque, Sami and Yasmin, above n 77.

82 *The Arbitration Act 2001* (Bangladesh) s. 23(1)(a)(b).

83 Noor Mohammad and Rakiba Nabi, *Enforcement of foreign arbitral awards concerning commercial disputes in Bangladesh: A brief overview* <https://doi.org/10.1108/08288660810917150> 1st June 2024.

84 *Arbitration Act* 2001 (Bangladesh), s. 46(b) (ii).

85 Faruque, Sami and Yasmin, above n 77, 116.

86 *Saipem v Bangladesh*, above n 9, para 3–37.

87 In *Saipem v Bangladesh*, Bangladesh, as the respondent, argued that the rights resulting from an ICC award concerning a contractual dispute would not fall within the investment notion of a pertinent investment treaty between Bangladesh and Italy, the home state of Saipem (see *Saipem v Bangladesh*, para 127).

88 See Lindsay Marchassault, '*Chevron Bangladesh Block Twelve Ltd and Chevron Bangladesh Block Thirteen and Fourteen Ltd. v The People's Republic of Bangladesh*' (2010) ICSID Case No. ARB/06/10: Introductory Note (2011) 26(1) *ICSID Review* 256, 260–261.

89 See Lindsay Marchassault, '*Chevron Bangladesh Block Twelve Ltd and Chevron Bangladesh Block Thirteen and Fourteen Ltd. v The People's Republic of Bangladesh*' (2010) ICSID Case No. ARB/06/10: Introductory Note (2011) 26(1) *ICSID Review* 256, 260–261.. The tribunal decided this matter in consideration of the *Salini criteria*. See *Salini Costruttori S.p.A and Italstrade S.p.A v. Kingdom of Morocco* (2001) ICSID Case No. ARB/00/4 42 ILM 609.

90 HT Correspondent, Bangladesh wins arbitration on dispute with Chevron (*Hindustan Times*, 18 May 2010).

7 Conclusion

This book outlines the crucial role of foreign direct investment (FDI) in developing least-developed countries such as Bangladesh. It emphasises the need for development-oriented regulation to ensure sustainable development through FDI, highlighting the importance of proper regulation in areas such as entry, tax, environmental protection and labour rights. The book also underlines the necessity of balancing liberalisation and regulation to address the differing interests of investors and host countries.

The report highlights that Bangladesh has minimal entry regulations for foreign investment approval, reflecting a liberal approach to encouraging foreign investment. The country's regulations or policies do not specify specific requirements for local content, employment or technology transfer. Bangladesh allows 100 per cent equity participation without conditions and has few requirements for joint-venture investments. However, product-sharing contracts with foreign oil companies stipulate technology transfer and other requirements.[1]

The regulation of FDI operations to protect the environment is very important for achieving sustainable development. There is a growing concern about the environmental performance of multinational corporations involved in FDI, especially in developing host countries. However, the legal framework in Bangladesh lacks sufficient principles and mechanisms for environmental regulation, resulting in ineffective enforcement. The Ministry of Environment and Forest and the Department of Environment lack coordination and institutional capacity to address environmental problems effectively. Additionally, the judicial mechanism established by the Environment Court Act 2000 has limited scope for individuals due to bureaucratic intervention.

Bangladesh's current labour rights protection laws are not strong or sufficient compared to international standards. Due to certain restrictions, there are shortcomings in terms of freedom of association, collective bargaining and employment equality in the workplace. Although the legal framework for occupational safety and health (OSH) seems comprehensive, it does not fully comply with international standards, and there are discrepancies between laws and their enforcement. The measures to ensure compliance and enforcement

DOI: 10.4324/9781003469117-7

mechanisms are not robust enough to protect labour and employment rights. The internal monitoring and inspection processes are uncoordinated and inadequately staffed, and there is no requirement for periodic monitoring in the legal framework. Furthermore, judicial procedures are time-consuming and biased towards employers. The laws for workers in export processing zones (EPZs) do not fully recognise their right to freedom of association, collective bargaining and the international standards for setting minimum wages. The law even does not allow for the establishment of a labour court, and workers have little trust in the current arbitration system for resolving disputes with their employers.

Bangladesh currently lacks a specific policy or legal framework for involuntary resettlement. The existing legal framework established by the Acquisition and Requisition of Immovable Property Ordinance (ARIPO)1982 does not prioritise protecting rights related to involuntary resettlement. It has legal gaps in accordance with international human rights standards, particularly concerning the prior consent of affected persons for relocation, adequate rehabilitation and compensation measures. The law under ARIPO restricts the right to access justice by imposing limitations on judicial remedy in dispute resolution related to compensation. Similarly, the special legislations of the Chittagong Hill Tract district do not focus on the participation of Indigenous people in the acquisition or requisition of their land or industrial plot allotment. The legal protection of FDI involves two main elements: protection against illegal expropriation and protection through dispute settlement mechanisms. The protection regime for foreign investment in a country should be formulated to accommodate the interests of host states. The study finds that the expropriation principle under the Foreign Private Investment Act (FPIA) of 1980, although not very categorical or comprehensive, creates a check and balance between the interests of investors and host states as it provides a wide range of prohibitions and conditional permissions. However, in the case of conditional permission, the law still follows the contentious and traditional "Hall formula", which was historically designed to protect the interests of the North investors. Therefore, the principle relating to compensation requires a change in the calculation method of the amount in consideration of host state interests at a given time.

The FDI legislation in Bangladesh does not provide a specific dispute settlement mechanism, and there are no clear policy guidelines in this regard. The dispute resolution options are usually determined through bilateral investment treaty (BIT) negotiations or individual investment contracts with foreign parties. Typically, most BITs in Bangladesh offer three common options for dispute resolution: conciliation, litigation in local courts or arbitration and international arbitration, to be pursued in sequence. However, foreign investors are hesitant to use local courts or arbitration in case of conflicting interests and generally prefer international arbitration. Conversely, the Bangladesh government, or any local partner of foreign investors, is often unwilling to resort to international arbitration, claiming that it favours the investors and overlooks the development interests of the host state. In such a scenario, there is a need to introduce a binding provision for dispute settlement, with a prerequisite of exhausting local remedies based on mutual agreement of the parties.

FDI is crucial for the overall development of Bangladesh. However, the country has experienced a decline in its FDI inflow in recent years. In 2023, Bangladesh received $3.004 billion in FDI, a decrease of 14 per cent from $3.5 billion in 2022. According to Bangladesh Bank, the net FDI inflow declined by 13.80 per cent in 2023 compared to the previous year. This has raised serious concerns about the country's ability to attract international capital for economic development. There are several reasons for such a decline, including macroeconomic challenges, such as volatility in the exchange rate, fall in foreign currency reserves, import compressions and production disruption. Weaknesses in the business climate, trade policy, logistics sector and outdated regulatory framework have also contributed to the decline in FDI.

The country's medium-term development plan aims to accelerate FDI flows by improving the investment climate and strengthening the Bangladesh Investment Development Authority (BIDA) capabilities to attract foreign investors. The government has established 100 economic zones (EZs) to encourage environment-friendly industrialisation and enhance domestic and foreign investment. To ensure that this will positively impact the country's development, it should also focus on revising its regulatory framework related to the operations of the FDI. For instance, the Board of Investment (BoI) and Bangladesh Export Processing Zones Authority (BEPZA), as administering agencies for foreign investment, should adopt a concrete screening policy to approve the FDI proposal. The screening policy must pursue the considerations as suggested in section 3 of the Foreign Private Investment (Promotion and Protection) Act 1980, including the possibility of foreign investment to contribute to employment opportunities, development of capital, technical and managerial resources, discovery and better utilisation of natural resources and strengthening the balance of payment and economic development of the country on the whole. The screening must consider the impact of foreign investment on the local economy. Another example is that the provision for the permission of free repatriation of profits under section 8 of the Foreign Private Investment (Promotion and Protection) Act 1980 should be modified with the condition of "after payment of corporate income tax and the fulfillment of other financial obligations". The tax may be any percentage of the profit transferred depending on the level of capital contribution of such investors from their source (home country and loan abroad) to the enterprise. The amount of reinvestment will not be taxable, and during the tax exemption period, the profit transfer should be conditional with re-investment in the project or specific ratio. The issue of repatriation in the event of liquidation should be added as a legal provision in the Foreign Private Investment (Promotion and Protection) Act 1980 with the requirement of compliance with the existing Company Act 1994 provision. In addition, under section 8(2) of the Foreign Private Investment (Promotion and Protection) Act 1980, the phrase "exceptional financial and economic difficulties" needs to be categorically defined to be consistent with commonly used international terminologies in the said respect.

FDI in Bangladesh has contributed to its economic development; these investments could further contribute to the country's overall development, including the development of the environment, human resources and national security. A well-thought regulatory framework can assist the country in maximising the capacity of FDI to ensure sustainable development. This text highlights the state of FDI regulation in Bangladesh. A comprehensive and all-inclusive study is needed to pinpoint the areas Bangladesh should focus on to revive its FDI-related regulatory framework and ensure the maximum benefits of FDI. I look forward to providing such an inclusive study soon, underlining the importance of thorough research in this field.

Note

1 See Bangladesh Oil, Gas and Mineral Corporation (Petrobangla), *Model Product-Sharing Contract* (2008) <http://www.eisourcebook.org/cms/Model%20Production%20Sharing%20Contract%20PETROBANGLA%202008.pdf> 10 June 2024.

Index

Note: Page numbers followed by "n" refer to end notes.

For Product Safety Concerns and Information please contact our EU representative GPSR@taylorandfrancis.com
Taylor & Francis Verlag GmbH, Kaufingerstraße 24, 80331 München, Germany

www.ingramcontent.com/pod-product-compliance
Lightning Source LLC
LaVergne TN
LVHW010932110826
845149LV00013B/2566

* 9 7 8 1 0 3 2 7 4 4 1 6 2 *